RESILIENCY AND SUCCESS

MIGRANT CHILDREN IN THE UNITED STATES

D0223585

RESILIENCY AND SUCCESS

MIGRANT CHILDREN IN THE UNITED STATES

ENCARNACIÓN GARZA

PEDRO REYES

ENRIQUE T. TRUEBA

PARADIGM PUBLISHERS

Boulder • London

Copyright © 2004 by Paradigm Publishers

Published in the United States by Paradigm Publishers, 3360 Mitchell Lane, Suite C, Boulder, Colorado 80301 USA.

Paradigm Publishers is the trade name of Birkenkamp & Company, LLC, Dean Birkenkamp, President and Publisher.

Library of Congress Cataloging-in-Publication Data

Garza, Encarnación, 1950–
Resiliency and success : migrant children in the United States / Encarnación Garza, Pedro Reyes, and Enrique T. Trueba.
p. cm.
ISBN 1-59451-044-x (hardcover : alk. paper) — ISBN 1-59451-045-8 (pbk. : alk. paper)
1. Children of migrant laborers—Education—United States. 2. Mexican Americans—Education. 3. Mexicans—Education—United States. I. Reyes, Pedro, 1954– II. Trueba, Enrique T., 1931– III. Title.

LC5151.G37 2004
371.826'24—dc22

2004001901

Printed and bound in the United States of America on acid-free paper that meets the standards of the American National Standard for Permanence of Paper for Printed Library Materials.

Designed and Typeset by Straight Creek Bookmakers.

09   08   07   06   05   04
5   4   3   2   1

CONTENTS

Contents

Contents

PREFACE

⊷

AWARENESS IS MEANINGLESS UNLESS IT INSPIRES AND IS FOLLOWED BY CHANGE. This study was about a long-ignored and yet well-researched group of people. The image of this group has been constructed in a way that locks them in a perpetuating cycle of failure. Consequently, many educators are convinced that the children of farm workers (the "ghost workers") will never be able to fly to high-achieving positions. Sadly, many of these students are led to believe that they are intrinsically inferior, or that it is their fate to follow the path of hopelessness that has been imposed on them for generations.

The attrition rates among the migrant student population have been phenomenal, and we know enough about the factors that contribute to this failure. Educational practitioners have been exposed sufficiently to this type of research. It is here precisely where the problem rests. The subliminal messages about the alleged inability of Hispanic children to succeed in schools are abundant and frequent. However, in spite of these predominant messages, there are many stories of success that have not been told.

With this in mind, the main purpose of this study was to elucidate the amazingly successful life journeys of academically invulnerable migrant students. One of the goals of this study was to invite readers, educational practitioners, policymakers, and researchers to transition from a primary phase of awareness to a more advanced phase of transformation and commitment to change. It is critical to use this awareness and sensitivity in a way that generates significant changes in attitude and behavior. We want to raise the expectations of educators about the talents, capabilities, and competence of migrant students.

Who are these children? In many cases these students have been referred to as the "invisible children," or the children of "ghost workers." Being invisible is not the worst of circumstances because it at least implies that they exist, even if they cannot be seen. However, in other instances, they are not even acknowledged. They are treated as if they do not exist at all. This mystery child is known as the "migrant student." There is a misconception that because of technological advances in agriculture, migrant farm workers are being displaced. Educators need to accept that this special population is increasingly growing in numbers. These students have long been in our schools and will continue to be there for a long time.

The literature is rich with accounts about the plight and demise of the Hispanic migrant student. Many studies have been conducted to explain why so many Hispanic students are failing in schools. Their poor achievement record has been consistently linked to a variety of sociocultural factors that compel Mexican American students to academic failure. The assumption of these findings is that the Hispanic child does not have the necessary competencies, values, and personal characteristics to succeed in America's schools.

Though Hispanics long preceded the present dominant group, they have remained foreign in their communities and invisible in their schools. Historically, they have not been expected to become participating members of the American way of life (Carter & Segura, 1979). The following quote illustrates similar views from a teacher in the Rio Grande Valley in the 1960s:

They are a good people. Their only handicap is the bag full of superstitions and silly notions they inherited from México. When they get rid of these superstitions they will be good Americans. The schools help more than anything else. In time, the Latinos will think and act like Americans. A lot depends on whether we can get them to switch from Spanish to English. When they speak Spanish they think Mexican. When the day comes that they speak English at home like the rest of us they will be part of the American way of life. I just don't understand why they are so insistent on using Spanish. They should realize that it's not the American tongue. These children may seem backward at first but it's not their fault. They just don't understand what is being said in class. They are bright but they don't speak our language. (Madsen, 1966, p. 106)

By focusing on the reasons for failure of Hispanic students in a system designed for mainstream white upper- and middle-class children, these types of studies have failed to generate effective long-term solutions. These students have been placed in demeaning and stigmatizing remedial pullout programs that have served to perpetuate negative teacher attitudes and low expectations about Hispanic students.

Not much emphasis has been given to Hispanic students who have overcome the obstacles and barriers impeding success. Little is known about the Hispanic student who is academically invulnerable (Alva & Padilla, 1995). If little is known about the successful Hispanic student, much less is known about academically successful Hispanic migrant children in U.S. schools. To address this problem, we have undertaken this project to probe into the lives of academically invulnerable Hispanic migrant students.

Why Is This Study Significant?

We have approached the study of migrant students from an ethnographic perspective, using qualitative approaches that require fine-tuned analysis of ethno-historical and interview data. We feel that this approach is essential to understand modern American society and its schools. We must first understand immigrant families and their children, who constitute the greatest portion of new students in the largest cities of this country. We cannot begin to plan appropriate pedagogical approaches for migrant students until we realize that (a) they are here to stay, (b) we know very little about them, and (c) their home language and culture are being discarded by schools, and educators are losing the most powerful means to reach these students. According to Alva and Padilla (1995), most of the current research of Hispanic students has focused on how sociocultural factors contribute to their failure in school. These studies have helped to develop and to justify acceptance of the dangerous and damaging deficit model. In educational circles, this model is often referred to as the culturally different paradigm. It is accepted by many teachers and condoned by many school administrators as a way to explain why minority students fail to perform according to standards.

Many educators assume that the failure of Hispanic students in school and their subsequent poverty can be naturally attributed to their racial or cultural inferiority. Much of the literature has focused on the alleged deficiencies of the Hispanic child, fostering attitudes of racial prejudice (Carter & Segura, 1979). Teachers have been reading such literature for a long time. For example, Gamio (1930/1971) wrote, "The mental capacity of the Mexican child is probably normal, although some investigators conclude that he is mentally inferior to an American child of the same age" (p. 72). In another study conducted by Taylor (1934), a teacher commented, "Some Mexicans are very bright, but you can't compare their brightest with the average white children. They are an inferior race" (p. 202). In dealing with culturally different students, schools historically have either ignored them or have imposed upon them a curriculum designed to eradicate their identities and "Americanize" them.

There are several implications inherent in this paradigm. The most obvious one is that accepting cultural difference as an excuse for failure implies that children who are culturally different are inherently less competent, less intelligent, less capable, and less motivated than the children of the more affluent, dominant culture. It suggests that unless they change their culture, values, and physical appearance, they have little or no chance to be successful in school. Teachers who accept this paradigm are also saying that nothing is wrong with their pedagogy, teaching practices, methodologies, or with the school system. Therefore, they will continue to operate the same way and students must learn to adapt to the programs available to them or fail. According to this approach, the solution for improvement is beyond the teachers' and school system's realm of influence and power.

Alva and Padilla (1995) suggested that there is a dire need for "multivariate paradigms" to guide educational research dealing with Mexican American students. This study examined how sociocultural, personal, and environmental factors interact to influence the academic performance of the successful migrant students. It will potentially provide educators and policy makers with important information about the coping resources related to success rather than the risk factors associated with failure. Finally, we must draw important theoretical and methodological lessons from this study of the unexpected success of the children of "ghost workers."

ACKNOWLEDGMENTS

↭

The lives and education of migrant farm worker children, their parents and their families has always been a topic of intense passion in our lives. Given the pervasiveness of the deficit thinking in educational settings, migrant children are confronted with a phenomenal challenge to overcome the low expectations bestowed upon them by teachers and the educational system in general. This book defies and debunks the myth that migrant children are doomed to failure because of their lifestyle. This study illustrates poignantly how migrant students who succeed in school "beat the system" because of their migrant lifestyle—not in spite of it.

I want to express special thanks to my mother, Consuelo Garcia Garza, and my father, the late Encarnación Garza. *Madre, muchas gracias por su apoyo y amor. Todo se lo debo a usted y a mi padre. Siempre fué un sacrificio para ustedes pero nunca dejaron de apoyarnos. Su ilusión siempre me dió gran esperanza. Desde el primer dia que me mandó a la escuela, hasta esta fecha, su gran orgullo ha sido una inspiración. Muchas gracias.* My parents could not help me with my schoolwork, and I depended on my older brother, Jaime and sister, Oralia. I thank them dearly. As a family, we worked together to survive. Thank you Magdalena, Juan, and Jorge. Special thanks to my wife, Rebecca, for her support and input as she read and edited my work every step along the way to the final draft. Finally, special thanks to the most important people in my life, my daughters Alissa and Alejandra, and my granddaughter, Anayi. I dedicate this book to the memory of my daughter, Alejandra "Landi" Garza. She is forever in my heart and continues to be my inspiration.

Encarnación Garza

I would like to thank my wife, Gloria C. Reyes, for all the understanding and love she demonstrated as we worked on this book. I also want to thank my children, Pedro Jr., Damian, Jaine, Yulissa, and Yessenia Reyes. They have been a source of inspiration for me.

Pedro Reyes

I would like to thank all the families who participated in this study. They are a source of pride and inspiration to all of us. Thank you to Encarnación and Pedro for working together on this incredible project.

Enrique Trueba

I
THE IMMIGRATION EXPERIENCE AND RESILIENCY OF MEXICAN FAMILIES IN THE UNITED STATES

OVER THE LAST DECADE, ONE OF THE MOST IMPORTANT DEVELOPMENTS IN THE United States has been that of immigration. Thousand of immigrants have settled in the U.S. and have brought in their families or developed new families. According to scholars,

> immigration is the driving force behind a significant transformation of American society. In 1945, just fifty years ago, the U.S. population was 87% White, 10% Black and 2.5% Hispanic and .5% Asian. In the year 2050, the projection of the demographics of the U.S. will be 52.8% White, 13.6% Black, 24.5% Hispanic, 8.2% Asian. (Suárez-Orozco, 1998a, b, p. 6)

The impact caused by immigrant populations in our society and schools begins to be understood. Immigration has emerged as an important topic of global concern. Since 1965, the United States has formally admitted over twenty million new immigrants. The vast majority of new immigrants to the United States are non-English speaking people of color coming from the Afro-Caribbean basin, Asia, and Latin America. Moreover, new research has suggested that there are 2–4 million "undocumented" immigrants living in the United States; an estimated 200,000–400,000 undocumented immigrants enter the United States every year. Thus, immigrant children are the fastest growing sector of the U.S. child population.

This tremendous growth has significant implications for schools and society. Thus, this chapter explores in detail the issues and challenges associated with immigrants in the United States. Specifically, we analyze the context of migration to the United States. We review some of the challenges they face, and speculate on the factors that define the experiences of immigrants and how they survive in a world that is foreign to them. Finally, we explain why a significant number of immigrants succeed in spite of the obstacles they face in the United States. We focus primarily on immigrants of Mexican descent.

The Context of Mexican Immigration

The problems faced by Mexicans in what is today the United States did not start with the tens of thousands who came to do unskilled labor in the late 1800s. Certainly, many Mexicans were living in the Southwest prior to the annexation of Mexican territory by the Guadalupe Hidalgo Treaty of 1848, but many more have come since. The economic opportunities of North America have attracted Mexicans in search of employment in increasing numbers since the beginning of the 20th century. The U.S. Census of 1900 estimated that there were 103,393 Mexican immigrants. By 1910, there were 221,915; by 1920, 486,418, and by December 31, 1926, the official count was 890,746 (Gamio, 1930/1971).

Scholars have emphasized the significance of Mexican immigration in the entire immigration patterns of the last three decades. The rising numbers of legal and unauthorized immigrants and political refugees represent a pattern that is changing the texture of American democracy, the ethnic and racial composition of U.S. cities, and popular culture. The Mexican-origin population has grown at a steady and fast pace since 1980. Part of this growth is understandable because of the higher fertility rates of Mexicans (35–40% higher than those of Anglos) and the total number of children in Mexican families. Without immigration, in 1990 the total Mexican-origin population (the sum of the Mexican-born population and U.S. natives of Mexican parentage) would have been about 14% of its current size. This increase is clearly the primary result of immigration (González Baker, Bean, Escobar Latapí & Weintraub, 1998). The steady stream of immigrants from Mexico, along with other Latino immigrants, has become the single largest continental proportion (nearly 38%) of legal immigrants and an estimated 80% of undocumented immigrants.

All factors indicate that this flow of Mexican immigrants will continue at a rapid pace. Foreign-born persons of Mexican origin in 1980 constituted 15% of all legal immigrants; in 1990, 20.7%; in 1994–1995, 28.4%. The increase of the Mexican population in the United States between 1960 and 1996 is as follows: 1960, 1.7 million (1% of the total U.S. population); 1970, 4.5 million (2.2%); 1980, 8.7 million (3.9%); 1990, 13.3 million (5.4%); 1995, 17 million (6.6%); and 1996, 18 million (6.7%).

It is significant that the 6.8 million Mexicans born in Mexico and living in the United States constitute 38.2% of the total Mexican population and 25.8% of all the foreign born persons. Furthermore, between 1980 and 1996, 1.8 million became naturalized citizens (González Baker et al., 1998). In 1996, 12.4% of the total Mexican population in the U.S. was foreign born, and in 1996 alone 851,803 persons from Mexico became naturalized citizens of the United States. The number of estimated undocumented Mexicans in the United States in 1995 was 2.1 million (González Baker et al.).

Sixty percent of Mexican immigrants live in California. As has been recognized, a person's educational level seems to predict economic level and employment. The highest rates of poverty are found among the populations with the least education—Mexicans, Salvadorians, Guatemalans, and Dominicans. New immigrant children face many difficult problems in their adaptation (U.S. Bureau of the Census, 1996). What has prompted this immigration to the United States?

At least three important economic factors influence immigration. According to Enrique Dussel Peters (2000), Mexico's principal strategy to improve its economy has been control of the inflation rate and the fiscal deficit, as well as import liberalization and the attraction of foreign investments. Accordingly, these changes are supposed to stimulate incentives for economic restructuring. Second, the Banco de México pursued orthodox and restrictive monetary and credit policies to achieve the main objectives of the strategy. The nominal exchange rate was used as an anchor to control inflation, which resulted in a depreciation of the exchange rate. Third, México approved the implementation of the North American Free Trade Agreement on January 1, 1994. Accordingly, this strategy brought inflation and the fiscal deficit under control until 1994, and the country attracted massive foreign investment. However, the economy has not been able to integrate its growing population into formal employment. In fact, the Mexican economy not only has failed to integrate the growing economically active population but also has massively ex-pelled labor power from several activities. Dussel Peters (2000) indicated that "employment growth [during 1988–1994] has been far below the levels achieved before 1982." In sum, this strategy resulted in an in-creasing social, economic, and regional polarization, because only a few branches and export-oriented sectors have been able to benefit from these policies.

> Neither employment nor real wages in Mexico are the only causes of immigration to the United States, it is at least possible to say that there is a vast potential of labor power in Mexico that is willing to work and desperate enough to join the informal labor market and to cross the border to the United States. The increasing gap in GDP between Mexico and the United States since the 1980s seems to sharpen this tendency. (p. 71)

On the other side, the economic demand for Mexican workers along with the economic needs of Mexican families have jointly resulted in the increase of Mexican immigrants. The shift from agricultural (often sea-sonal) jobs to urban, more stable employment (a pattern in previous decades when U.S. employers closed unionized plants and opened up new ones) gave Mexican-immigrant supervisors the responsibility of hir-ing and firing portions of the workforce. This increased the numbers of kin and countrymen in the plants. The 1986 Immigration Reform and Control Act (IRCA) legalized many of the undocumented immigrants and permitted them to bring their families. This migration, then, has produced significant stressors.

Immigration Stressors

In the United States, most Latino families live in urban centers (U.S. Bureau of the Census, 1990). The first challenge for them is survival. Although most enter legally, many stay past their legal time period in order to work and to support their families. Those without proper doc-umentation live in constant fear of discovery and are ready victims for exploitation (Smolowe, 1997).

The immigrant who comes to the United States from a rural village or small town in Mexico or Latin America is often completely overwhelmed by the contrasts found in modem U.S. cities. In many Latino communities, the cultural worldview of the church, the society, and the school are all one and the same. The major institutions are in agreement about who you are and how you are to live your life. This is changing in the larger Latin American cities, to the dismay of many Latinos.

The process of leaving their familiar homeland, family, and friends is often a traumatic experience occasioned by economic or political necessity and dreams of a better life. Crossing the border without documentation can be dangerous and expensive. Many have been robbed, raped, beaten, and left for dead in their effort to cross to the United States. Many Central Americans come to the United States traumatized by war and suspicious of all government officials. Some estimate that one out of every three who cross the border illegally is caught and sent back.

The acculturation process involves acquisition of language and the predominant values and behaviors of the host society. This process is also a source of distress. The importance of the home language for the psychological survival of Mexican immigrants cannot be overemphasized. Their ability to retain a measure of self-identity and personal integrity, to communicate and to pass on to the next generation their values and lifestyle, depends on their ability to retain the home language. The native languages, cultures, religions, art, values, lifestyle, family organization, children's socialization patterns, and worldview constitute the survival kit for many immigrants. It is through language and communication that immigrants stay connected to their home country and ancestors (Delgado-Gaitan & Trueba, 1991; Hondagneu-Sotelo, 1994; Trueba, 1999; Trueba, Cheng & Ima, 1993; Trueba, Jacobs & Kirton, 1990; Trueba, Rodríguez, Zou & Cintrón, 1993, Trueba & Zou, 1994).

Immigrants often see the worse parts of American society: the slums, the back alleys, the inhumane living conditions of farm workers, the backbreaking jobs that no one else wants. The immigrant experience of America is often one that is without mercy, without justice, without compassion. With time, some may see a different picture of the United States. They can see that there is also a lot that is good in the United States, and that their experience of the shadow side of our society is one-sided. This is best expressed by immigrants who have been in the United States for many years and who have been able to make a living and support a family. There is a sense of thankfulness for a chance to make a better life than was possible in their homeland.

Also, immigrants experience significant prejudice attached to their race and ethnicity. They are forced to become experts in psychological and economic survival by adapting to a new life style and acquiring second and third languages. America's obsession with race and ethnicity feeds the obvious anxiety about the increasing waves of immigrants of color, especially Asians and Latinos. Thus, race and ethnicity continue to be at the center of public discourse and political debate. McLaren (1995) described how the American "predatory culture" configures public discourse and modern life in order to pursue the exploitation of less technologically developed individuals:

> In our hyper-fragmented and predatory postmodern culture, democracy is secured through the power to control consciousness and semioticize and discipline bodies by mapping and manipulating sounds, images and information and forcing identity to take refuge in the forms of subjectivity increasingly experienced as isolated and separate from larger social contexts. (p. 117)

Race and ethnicity will determine a person's relative status and chances for success. Race and ethnicity can predict residential information, and residence can predict educational achievement, income, dropout rates and suspension rates, size of family, mortality trends, incarceration, tendencies to violence, and use of welfare. The American banking policies, justice system, investment policies, and even the distribution of resources and liabilities (from the location of banks, grocery stores, movie theaters to that of waste disposal, prisons, and nuclear sites) use that information to make decisions. As Ladson-Billings and Tate (1995) have emphasized, social class and gender considerations alone "are not powerful enough to explain all the difference (or variance) in school experience and performance" and consequently "race continues to be a significant factor in determining inequity in the United States" (p. 48–49). Then, schools become the only vehicle to achieve mobility in the social and economic strata. What challenges do immigrant children face in American schools?

School Performance of Mexican Children

By the year 2030, White students will constitute about 30% of the total public school enrollment and Latino students will represent the largest group, 44% of the total enrollment (Valencia, 1991). Other school de-mographic projections suggest that the White school-age population will decrease in the United States, while the Latino school-age population will continue to increase. Latino children (5–17 years of age) numbered 6 million in 1982 (9% of the national youth population); by 2020 they will increase to 19 million (25%). The Latino school-age population will triple in 28 years (Valencia). Foreign-born persons of Mexican origin in 1980 represented 15% of the U.S. population; in 1990, 20.7%; and in 1995, 28.7% (González Baker et al., 1998). This trend, often called the "brownization" of North America, has raised fears in some that the new immigrants, now at the bottom of the economic ladder, may remain unassimilated in enduring pockets of poverty.

Much of the future of these immigrants depends on schools, and according to some researchers (Orfield & Eaton, 1996), schools are not ready to handle this problem. According to the Harvard Project on Desegregation (Orfield, Bachmeier, James & Eitle, 1997), between 1970 and 1994 Latino school enrollment has increased significantly in Califor-nia, Texas, New York, Florida, Illinois, Arizona, New Mexico, and New Jersey. Additionally, the isolation of Latinos has increased.

According to C. Suárez-Orozco and M. Suárez-Orozco (1995a, 1995b), and Suárez-Orozco (1998a, 1998b), immigrants must face at the same time problems of stress, housing, and racism. M. Suárez-Orozco and Suárez-Orozco (1995b) explained as follows:

> The obvious difficulties that most migrants face include language in-adequacies, a general unfamiliarity with the customs and expectations of the new country, limited economic opportunities, poor housing conditions, discrimination, and what psychologists term the "stresses of acculturation"....Despite these obstacles, many migrants often con-sider their lot as having improved from what it was in their country of origin. Because of a perception of relative improvement, many mi-grants may fail to internalize the negative attitudes of the host country toward them, maintaining their country of origin as a point of refer-ence. (p. 325)

Indeed, immigrants hold their belief of improvement by visiting their villages of origin and displaying some wealth conspicuously (showing new trucks, good clothes, and spending money). The Suárez-Orozcos

(1995b) have suggested that immigrants do not see their new life in terms of the ideals of the majority society but in terms of the "old culture," thus holding to a "dual frame of reference" (p. 325).

Parents' naïve notions about the politics of employment, organization, and politics in schools; their perception of societal demands for cultural homogenization; and the acceptance of an inferior status are not shared by their children. Their children feel an ethical responsibility to react and fight back. Much of what happens in gang struggles and street violence is related to marginalization (Vigil, 1989, 1997).

Many Mexican families reflect in their new lives a change not only from one country to another, but also from a rural to an urban setting. The added dimension in the United States is that in order to acquire the necessary sociopolitical knowledge of appropriate conduct in urban settings, immigrants must first acquire communicative skills in a second language. Unfortunately, Mexican immigrants are forced to take jobs that are physically exhausting and leave them little time to acquire communicative skills in English. Consequently, children (as soon as they learn some English) must play adult roles in making momentous decisions for their parents. Mexican immigrant children who are socialized in a new linguistic and cultural environment without help in the development of second-language skills and cognitive abilities required for high school achievement. As the popular song goes, "*el gringo terco a sacarnos y nosotros a volver* [the gringo is stubborn to get us out and we are stubborn to return]."

Narratives of academic achievement often represent a surprising success where failure was expected. It seems that the retention of the home language and the acquisition of the second language, if accompanied by high literacy levels in both English and Spanish, constitute a powerful factor affecting the successful adaptation of Mexican immigrants and their understanding of the complex U.S. social, economic, and political systems. Their ability to handle text related to those systems for the family (contracts, government documents, bank documents, hospitals documents, immigration papers, and so on) is contingent upon their bilingualism and biliteracy.

On the other hand, the rapid marginalization of other Mexican families (especially youth) is accelerated by their problems understanding American institutions, accompanied by the lack of literacy and language proficiency skills in both languages. This marginalization often starts long before they arrived to this country. Their naïve notions about the politics of employment, the organization of schools, the demands of society, and the legal and economic system often result in tragic consequences: incarceration, loss of income, ignorance of civil rights, and other abuses. The lack of linguistic and literacy skills may reflect an abrupt transition from rural to urban settings, from simple village life to the life in the large metropolis. This transition is accompanied by culture shock and deterioration in mental health.

Another serious challenge facing Mexican immigrant families at their arrival is the isolation, neglect, and malnutrition experienced as they look for employment. As if this were not enough, the lack of legal documents is a source of anxiety every day with the increasing raids by the Immigration and Naturalization Service. They feel vulnerable but cannot seek help from social agencies, even if they qualify for assistance. Frequently, workers do not have health insurance or welfare, and they do not have access to a physician prior to or just after childbirth. The deplorable housing conditions (from shantytowns to crowded garages) increase the chances of health problems, child neglect, and child safety problems. In urban areas, the safety of the entire family is jeopardized in dilapidated, drug-infested housing. These conditions are also conducive to early recruitment of Mexican children into gangs and their school dropouts?.

The experiences of discrimination, of verbal and physical abuse on the part of mainstream children, and the predominant opinion among teachers that Mexican children are low achievers certainly does not help. These experiences create for immigrant children a difficult setting in which they must redefine themselves in the United States. In the search for a new personal identity, Mexican youth often feel pressure to reject their family, language, and culture. These symbolic "self-rejections" and the formation of a new cultural identity do not necessarily result in embracing North American values or higher levels of English literacy. The traumatic experience of being uprooted and the confusion about family values, personal survival, coupled with the need for peer support, is bound to lead many young people to become affiliated with gangs and to disregard the codes of behavior prescribed by mainstream society. In fact, the increasing marginalization of Mexican youth is reflected in the high rates of dropout and incarceration. A number of scholars have recently dealt with these problems of adaptation in the context of the school environment (Bartolomé, 1996; Bartolomé & Macedo, 1997; Delgado-Gaitan,

1994; Deyle & Margonis, 1995; Gutierrez, 1994; Patthey-Chavez, 1993; Wilson, 1991).

Research has shown an intimate relationship between the successful adaptation of Mexican immigrant families to U.S. society and the academic success of their children. For example, a recent study in central California (Trueba, 1999) showed that the most serious problem faced by the children of immigrants is the alienating experience of schooling; the rapid marginalization of these children; and their confusion regarding personal identity, cultural values, social acceptance, the ability to achieve, and overall self-worth. Consequently, if children manage to retain a strong self-identity and remain part of the sociocultural community, they can achieve well in school. Parents usually provide protection so that their children maintain their identity and cultural values.

For example, sometimes a Mexican family takes drastic measures to salvage the moral character and overall well-being of a youth by taking him or her back to Mexico for a period of time to complete his or her education, to re-acquire Spanish, to work under supervision, and even to marry. There are some cases when the entire family returns to the Mexico for an extended period of time (2 or 3 years) in order to re-educate teenagers in the family values. There are a number of repatriated ex-farmworkers in central Mexico (the states of Colima, Michoacán, and Jalisco). In contrast, many alienated Mexican immigrant children in major metropolises (e.g., Los Angeles, Chicago, New York, Houston), cannot manage to retain their home language and culture or their familiar cultural institutions and networks. Some seem to survive the trauma of American schooling and to achieve well.

Resiliency

Contrary to initial optimism and ethics of hard work, Mexican families do not always escape poverty. The number of children per immigrant family is higher than among other families. The economic and health needs of Mexican immigrant families are greater than those of families born and raised in the United States. Neither economic problems (often associated with the lack of steady employment) nor the frequent verbal abuse and prejudice of bosses and neighbors deter them. Mexican immigrants know they are tough and determined, and they are proud to survive in the worst of circumstances. These physically and spiritually strong individuals articulate their own voices and feel important individually and collectively. What makes these individuals succeed when they face tremendous challenges in the United States? We propose the concept of resiliency as a possible explanation.

The resiliency of Mexican families and communities is an important concept to understand this book. Its sociocultural and psychological basis and its intimate link to the collective commitment to maintaining their language and a sense of "community" are central to our discussion. Without this resiliency, children of Mexican immigrants would never understand the importance of their ethnic identity and their historical relationship with ancestors. Mexican immigrants are proud of retaining their language and culture.

Women's role in this retention process requires endurance and determination, as shown not only in their daily agricultural labor but also in their capacity to organize themselves into a political force to negotiate with the school and to fight for their children's education. They seem to learn quickly how American society functions. They also know how to motivate their children to achieve academically. Their apparent oppressive daily work in the fields and packing houses may be in clear contrast with their own self-worth and their enormous prestige in their home village in Mexico. They must work hard under precarious conditions that affect their health significantly; they suffer from arthritis, bronchitis, allergies, malnutrition, and high blood pressure. But this oppression does not seem to break their spirits or to jeopardize their determination to succeed.

What are the circumstances under which some families can do so much with so little, and continue to do more? What makes some members within a family more resilient to adversity and gives them strength?

Resilience is defined as the ability to confront and to resolve problems and the capacity to utilize personal or social resources to enhance limited possibilities (Cochran, 1992; Rutter, 1987). However, resilience does not ensure that all stressors will be resolved—people can be resilient in some circumstances and vulnerable in others. Factors identified with resilience include: (a) affectionate ties within the family, including a strong network support system of family and friends (b) the active search for external support systems, such as churches and other services (e.g., mental health services) and (c) personal characteristics. These factors generate self-esteem and self-efficacy while sustaining and reinforcing resilience.

Social Network Support

Families negotiate risk situations through the utilization of personal or societal resources. The presence of support networks has proven to be very beneficial. The social support provided by these networks of family and friends has been found to have positive effects on the health and well-being of the patient and the caregiver (Cohen & Syme, 1985). Relationships with kin, friends, and acquaintances form an interactive network exchange of goods, affection, and various types of support important for individuals and families. For example, studies have shown that these networks help families survive in times of harsh economic conditions (Stack, 1974). Other studies have indicated that the social support provided through networks reduces psychological distress (Gore, 1981; Hirsch, 1981). The role of networks is especially important among immigrants. The migration experience is a stressful experience, which affects each family member differently. The migrant typically enters society at the lower levels of the social strata, and primary group relationships are altered (i.e., separation of part or the total family).

Families are the starting point in all biography (Denzin, 1989b). How they contribute to the success or the failure of their children has been attributed to such differentials as disciplinary and parenting styles, socioeconomic status, the possession of cultural capital, and class lifestyles. Families are thought to have enormous influence on a student's success at school (Baumrind 1978; Clark, 1983; Hess & Holloway, 1984). The extent of this influence has been predicated on the fact that "American education is structured to serve children who have had the average family experience or better" (Comer, 1988, p. 28).

What usually happens to those who do not have this "average family experience" has been categorized with the problematic aspects of education, such as dropping out of school. Contradictions to the norm provide researchers with an opportunity to see what is different from the stereotypical images of failure or success.

Clark's (1983) study found that no matter whether the family units comprise one or two parents, are wealthy, or are welfare recipients, those with successful children have authoritative parenting styles. These parenting styles are warm yet provide rules and regulations which lead the children to secure and trusting relationships that are transferred to the school setting. Clark also noted that families whose children are low achievers in school have authoritarian (dominating and demanding) or permissive (inconsistent) parenting styles. Children in such families display a greater degree of despair, pathos, lethargy, and psychological confusion than do children from homes with authoritative parenting styles, and they transfer these characteristics to the school setting.

Middleton (1987), in an analysis of family and school, showed that the creation of cultural capital is fraught with contradictions. Cultural capital is the knowledge that children acquire from sources other than the school that enables them to survive in society and succeed in school. Middleton showed that family dynamics produce, for example, the sexual division of labor that also operates at school. One of the factors in success is having access to resources that provide the know-how to be successful in the formal system. Having access to resources wherever they exist is clearly important to success.

External Support

For the Hispanic population, religion has played a major role in its birth, history, culture, social life, and social institutions. Major historical events, such as the Spanish Inquisition and the Spanish conquest of the indigenous populations of the New World in the name of religion, have shaped the Hispanic population and its experience. Hispanic history and cultures are deeply rooted by religious dynamics and reflect the central role that religion has played in their development. Today, religion still plays an important role in the cultural and social lives of Hispanics in the United States. However, Hispanic religious life also reflects modern complexities and changes in a multicultural and increasingly religiously diverse society. Hispanics have begun to examine and to claim other religions, raising questions not only about Hispanic religious identity and life, but also about Hispanic ethnic identity and culture.

The immigrant who comes to the United States from a rural village or small town in Mexico or Latin America is often completely overwhelmed by the contrasts found in modem U.S. cities. When immigrants leave their home and come across the border, everything may be strange and unknown. One place with a certain familiarity, where there may be a lessening of that fear and anxiety, is in church. The church, the priest, and the Mass are all familiar to them. A welcoming church becomes an oasis away from the stresses of being in a foreign country. Although not all church communities are welcoming, in the last twenty years the Catholic church and other mainline churches have made a concerted effort to provide Spanish-language services for Latino immigrants.

Latinos are bound together by a common language and religious tradition. On one hand, they have inherited something of the Latino indigenous spirit of their parents and grandparents: trust in God, faith in goodness of life, and a confidence in the rewards given to those who are respectful and obedient to their elders. On the other hand, there is also an American spirit within them, that rugged individualism that calls each one to make it on their own; to soar solo and to establish their own career, family, and home; to live wherever the job takes them; and to expect and demand justice and fair play. The job, the career, and the possibility of wealth and status take on a sacred character.

Religion, for Latinos, is also a mechanism for survival. It is the way to understand and put order to their universe. Religious beliefs and practices are for Latinos, like for many other cultural groups, a way of looking at the world that has been passed down from one generation to the next in order to give meaning and purpose to living. It touches the very core of who they are and helps them understand, survive in, and thrive in the world around them.

The church for Latinos can be a supportive community in the midst of strangers. The growing number of small storefront churches is testimony to the fact that when Latinos do not feel welcome in the mainline churches, they will leave and start their own. The point here is not the worthiness of one church over another, but the desire of Latinos to belong to a supportive and affirming group. In a new land with strangers all around, a different language, and different cultural ways, Latinos find comfort in their local church, where, for a brief time, they feel at home. For the vast majority of Latinos, this is the Catholic Church. But as more mainline and evangelical churches reach out and offer services sensitive to the needs of Latinos, it is only natural for them to go where they feel most welcomed and most at home.

Personal Attributes

Garmezy and Rutter (1983) showed that a combination of personal attributes and environmental factors support resilience. They identified eight protective factors as softening the effects of risk. Resilient individuals had fewer and less long-lasting stressors in their lives than did those children who developed problems in later life. They had neither a criminal father nor a schizophrenic mother; they had easygoing temperaments, making parental criticism less likely; and they were female. Additionally, they had opportunities to assume responsibilities in school and thus achieved success; they had success, but not necessarily academic success at school; they had a warm, close relationship with an adult and thus had higher expectations; and they were planners with coping skills.

Garmezy and Rutter (1983) also found that protective factors form a triad of (a) *personality-disposition factors* that help children cope, (b) a *supportive family* environment in which at least one parent allows the child autonomy, and (c) an *external support system* that provides a model for positive values. They emphasized that human development is a dynamic process and that the human personality is a self-righting mechanism that engages in ongoing attempts to organize experience.

Protective-factor research has been influential in discovering what has eluded at-risk research. Many young people who suffer stressors in their lives do perfectly well, and some seem little affected by their experiences. For example, resilient children who have alcoholic parents do not develop problems with coping. Werner and Smith (1989) found behavioral characteristics that differentiate resilient children from children who develop problems with coping. These are characteristics of temperament that elicit positive attention from parents: at least average intelligence and communication skills, achievement orientation, a responsible, caring attitude, a positive self-concept, an internal locus of control; and a belief in self-help.

The second factor that can lead at-risk children to success is the *self-as-agent construct*, which proposes that the self is an active agent in the construction of one's success (or failure). How people react to their environment, what opportunities are afforded them, and how the environment is changed by the self-as-agent are important for this study.

Spiritual influences in the family include both positive and negative learned practices. The positive practices are those we learn from various spiritual disciplines or teachers: faith, prayer, meditation, healing ceremonies, or even positive thinking. (Cross, 1995)

II
MIGRANT FARM WORKERS AND THEIR CHILDREN

⤙

THE INFORMATION WE GATHERED THROUGH THE REVIEW OF THE LITERATURE IS extensive. As we present this information, we will also share some of our own experiences of this lifestyle to validate and complement this information. The review of the literature examines probable reasons for the conditions and plight of the migrant child. It speaks to the demands for school improvement and change to address the needs of these children. It identifies the attempts and efforts by federal and state agencies to provide an equal life chance opportunity for these children on the move.

To explain the migrant child's plight in educational settings, it is imperative to discuss the key elements and components. First, we identify the migrant farm workers and outline their role. Second, we discuss the migrant child and his/her educational experiences. Third, we analyze the educational system's impact on the migrant student. Fourth, we trace the evolution of the Migrant Education Program as mandated by the Elementary and Secondary Education School Act in 1965.

Role and Profile of the Migrant Farm Worker

Most of us go to the grocery store at least once a week. We spend some time in the produce section carefully selecting fresh vegetables and fruits. We might then make our way to the canned goods section and pick up some canned asparagus, spinach, corn, green beans, peaches, or pears. This is an experience most Americans take for granted. We expect to have a wide variety of fresh and canned fruits and vegetables to choose from at affordable prices. We give little thought to how these goods made their way to grocery store shelves.

The cycle of production and distribution is long and complex and depends totally on a vital group of individuals known as the migrant farm workers. This multi-billion dollar agriculture industry is highly dependent on the influx of migrant and seasonal farm workers. Contrary to what most people think, fruit and vegetable production has steadily increased over the last decade. Eighty-five percent of the fruits and vegetables produced in this country are hand harvested and/or cultivated. Though the role of the migrant farm worker is so critical, their wages are meager. The annual income for the majority of these workers is less than $7,500 (Effland, Hamm, & Oliveira, 1993). The average income for a migrant family of 5.3 members was about $5,500 in 1988 (De Mers, 1988).

According to Shotland (1989), estimates on the number of migrant farm workers vary because there is no official federal agency or office responsible for the collection of migrant demographics. Estimates of the farm worker population vary, but each year a huge group of workers and their families (between 3 and 5 million people) leave their homes to follow the crops *in almost every state in the nation*. Agricultural labor requirements in a given area may vary greatly between the different phases of planting, cultivating, harvesting, and processing. Although the migrant population is diverse and its composition varies from region to region, the vast majority of all migrant workers are minorities. According to the National Agricultural Workers Survey (National Commission on Migrant Education, 1992), migrant farm workers are predominantly male (82%), Hispanic (94%), born in México (80%), and married (52%) with children. Contrary to what the general public may believe, most migrant farm workers are either American citizens or are working in the country legally.

The life of the migrant family revolves around working and moving. Most live in poverty, in hunger, and are always uncertain about the next place they will go to find work. Day after day, migrant children watch their parents do backbreaking work, always stooping and always picking. They move from field to field, often county to county or to a new state. The children are hopelessly locked in the arms of this lifestyle of migrancy (Coles, 1971). The main reason these families move from one job to another is to try to better their economic situation.

These families migrate along well-established geographic routes. The three distinct streams are: the East Coast Stream, the Midcontinent Stream, and the West Coast Stream (Shotland, 1989). The East Coast Stream consists of American Blacks, Mexican Americans and Mexican nationals, Anglos, Jamaican and Haitian Blacks, and Puerto Ricans. This route includes the states along the eastern seaboard and the southern part of the United States. The Midcontinent Stream primarily consists of Mexican Americans and Mexican nationals, with small numbers of American Indians. The route begins in south Texas and moves north through the midwestern and western states. The Western Stream starts in California and moves up through Oregon and Washington. Although composed mostly of Mexican Americans and Mexican nationals, it has, in recent years, also included Southeast Asians (Shotland, 1989).

The Migrant Child's Educational Experience

Some of us in education have experienced the same lifestyle of the migrant children we serve. Somehow, a few of us were able to break out of this vicious cycle of poverty. We managed to survive in a system that was not designed to meet our basic needs as human beings. However, the vast majority of our classmates did not make it.

We remember working in the fields during many hot summer months, cold winter weekends, and many days after school. We knew of no type of work other than the fields. As many children of migrant farm workers today, we thought this was the only kind of work in the world. While all our friends were making plans for the summer, we dreaded the end of the school year. Our friends could not possibly understand why.

When we enrolled in college, our families no longer expected us to work in the fields from summer to summer. We completed our degrees quickly (three years) and ironically found ourselves in the fields once again. The difference this time was that we knew it was only a temporary assignment. Eventually, we got our first "real" jobs as teachers. It felt strange going from the "fields of dignity" to the classroom. As college students, the classroom kept us out of the fields during the summer, and as educators, the classroom has kept us away forever.

Throughout our careers, we have worked with many migrant children. One of us had the opportunity to work with summer migrant programs in the states of Colorado, Ohio, New York, Maine, Washington, Indiana,

Florida, and Montana. Lamentably, not much has changed for this hard-working and industrious group of students in schools or in the fields. It is hard but not impossible to understand the special experiences and needs of these children.

The following scenario depicts the painful experience of a student with whom one of us had the opportunity to work. Imagine that you are a migrant student at a middle school in the Rio Grande Valley. You and your family have been migrating to Minnesota ever since you can remember. You always enroll after school has started and leave before the school year is over. You have never had the opportunity to participate in anything other than the normal classroom activities. Worse, you have never felt welcomed or invited to participate. This year something is different; a special teacher has encouraged you to try out for the impromptu speaking team. You accept the challenge and work hard to make the team. You have never been involved in any competitive events before, much less won anything. Your confidence comes and goes, but the support of the coach keeps you focused. Your hard work pays off: you make the team and go on to win the district championship. It seems strange to be noticed and acknowledged suddenly by your teachers and peers. You go from being almost invisible to being one of the most recognized students on campus.

It is now the second semester and the school principal has asked you to deliver the promotion speech at the eighth-grade graduation ceremony. Winning the championship was exciting, but the invitation from the principal to be the main speaker is the greatest honor you have ever experienced. You are the happiest and proudest person in the world, and you can hardly wait to tell your parents about it. Abruptly, your parents shock you back to reality. They tell you that you will soon have to withdraw from school to go work in Minnesota again.

For the first time you feel cheated and resentful for being the son/daughter of a migrant farm worker. How naive of you to think that your parents would simply postpone their departure until late May. It is difficult and almost embarrassing to give your counselor and principal the bad news. The principal offers to pay for your airfare if your parents will let you stay with a relative until school lets out. Though you knew your parents will never allow it, you still ask, only to be disappointed again. That is the life of a migrant.

The preceding account is a true story and a common experience among thousands of migrant students enrolled in U.S. schools. This young woman is a recent graduate from St. Edward's University. Unfortunately, she is one of very few migrant students to have graduated from high school and gone on to college. A great number of migrant students are deprived of the experiences many other students and educators take for granted. Besides being excluded by the system, they do not participate because of transportation problems, work activities, after-school responsibilities, or simply because their parents are not aware of the extracurricular programs available.

The Migrant Student Record Transfer System (MSRTS) identified 628,150 migrant farmworkers' children in 1992 (MSRTS, 1992), and as many as 800,000 in 1994 (MSRTS, 1994). The number of migrant children rose by 17% during the 1980s. These children range between 3 and 21 years of age, and most of these children travel with their migrant parents and do agricultural work. Texas is second only to California in the number of migrant students served (National Commission on Migrant Education, 1992). In Texas, there are approximately 161,000 migrant students, of which 46,000 migrate to 42 different states throughout the country (TEA, 1995). They are the invisible children in schools and communities.

Migrant children's lives are affected by many things that surround them and their families. The circumstances of these children are particularly heartbreaking. Poverty and mobility are the two main factors that impact migrant children. They are the poorest, most impoverished and poorly nourished students. Though their parents play a critical role in bringing food to others' tables and labor in the midst of an abundance of food, it is ironic that many of their children suffer from malnutrition and often go to bed hungry (Shotland, 1989). The parents of these migrant children suffer humiliating experiences when they have to stand in line for food stamps in order to purchase the very food they have cheaply picked for the rest of the people in this country.

In addition to the problems associated with mobility and poverty, other impeding factors are language, culture, inconsistent record keeping, lack of academic skills, overage in grade placement, and the need to work or care for younger children. Migrant students and their families also face economic, cultural, and social discrimination (Chavkin, 1991). These children face many other hardships associated with their migrant lifestyle. Many still travel in tarp-covered trucks owned by labor contractors who transport them to their work destinations. They drive for long hours in pitiful, unsanitary conditions lacking bathroom facilities. Families stake claim to part of the truck bed and keep their belongings within this designated area. The trip itself is an ordeal, and once they reach their destinations, most of these children live in deplorable substandard housing at best.

Constant mobility makes it hard for farmworker children to complete their education. These students average two to three schools a year and are usually behind grade level 6–18 months. The median educational level for the head of a migrant family was 6 years in 1986 (Harrington, 1987). The research has shown that high mobility lowers student achievement, especially when it is coupled with poverty and living in uneducated, illiterate families. Consequently, these students have the highest failure and dropout rates (Straits, 1987). Migrant students have the lowest graduation rate of any population group in the public schools. Five times as many migrant students are enrolled in the second grade as in the 12th grade, and migrant educators place the dropout rate for migrant students anywhere from 50–90% (Interstate Migrant Education Council, 1987). The Migrant Attrition Project conducted a study that showed a 45% national dropout rate, whereas a study done 12 years earlier had reported a 90% dropout rate (Salerno, 1991).

It is not uncommon for a migrant child to be enrolled in school one week and gone the next. Many students leave school without making the proper withdrawal arrangements. Many parents of migrant students are forced to leave on a short notice from the labor contractors or growers. Efficient transfer of student records is a major problem; receiving schools may never get them or may have to wait 3–5 months for them. Without this information, often these students are held back or given inappropriate placement (Ascher, 1991). In many instances school officials refuse to admit these children to their schools due to lack of documentation. In spite of the *Plyler v. Doe* ruling in 1982 that specifically protected these children, schools in Texas and other states continue to violate their civil rights (Hunter & Howley, 1990).

The migrant family migrates to secure better job opportunities. Most families find themselves in dire financial stress just to meet basic survival needs. Consequently, education becomes a secondary priority. According to Prewitt-Díaz, Trotter, and Rivera (1989), the teenager who works in the fields gives 80% of his/her earnings to the family. In our own experiences we never even saw or knew how much we earned; 100% of our wages went to the family budget. The frequent change of environment keeps the migrant child in a continuous state of adjustment to school, friends, and language. These children are not accepted readily by school staff and classmates. The high percentage of dropouts among migrant students in many cases is due to their feelings of isolation. Because of insufficient attendance and lack of effective coordination between home base and receiving schools, the child's education is interrupted and fragmented (Harrington, 1987). Educational strategies, curriculum, and textbooks vary from school to school, and many times teachers are not willing to bother with a student who will be in their classrooms only a few weeks. As these children fall further behind, their self-concept is damaged. As a consequence, migrant children usually have very low self-esteem. Many times they are mistreated, embarrassed, and humiliated for speaking Spanish, dressing poorly, and simply being different and unique.

The Educational System

The educational system has been developed for and geared toward the White, middle-class, permanent community resident. It is evident that these special students present a challenging problem for schools. In the current system, migrant children immediately earn the labels of disadvantaged and at-risk. Many migrant children do not feel welcomed in schools. Because schools are not equipped to serve these children, many times these children are made to feel like they are a burden. In the recent past (and probably in some instances today), many schools and teachers placed these children in the back of the room and practically ignored them. If they were lucky, a teacher assistant may have been assigned to help them with busy and unchallenging work. A common strategy has been to refer migrant children to special education programs. This is a conspicuous form of tracking. It denies these children equal access to learning. Tracking perpetuates inequity and contributes to the continuing gaps in achievement between disadvantaged and affluent students and between minorities and Whites (Oakes, 1985).

Another widely used form of tracking with migrant students has been to group them according to their English language proficiency. We experienced this type of tracking over thirty years ago, and it is still a widely used practice. According to Braddock (1990), ability grouping increases when there are a high number of Black and Hispanic students enrolled. "The failure of such children can be attributed to a lack of compatibility between the characteristics of minority children and the characteristics of a typical instructional program" (Cardenas & Cardenas, 1977, p. 22). It is disturbing and somewhat terrifying to hear politicians and policymakers say that schools need to return to teaching the basics. Obviously, those who will be taught the basics will be the migrant and other disadvantaged students. Thus, the achievement gap will continue to grow and these students will continue to lag further behind. Migrant students must be challenged with higher expectations. "They need more from education than the basics. They need an education that can be related to everyday life, an education that will give them hope for a brighter future" (Dyson, 1983, p. 1).

It is evident that migrant children have not been afforded equal and equitable opportunities to be successful in America's schools. Whatever the reasons, and whether it has been done intentionally or unconsciously, the fact is that migrant children have been denied privileges that most mainstream American children enjoy.

A Compensatory Program: The Migrant Education Program

Until thirty years ago, no programs existed to compensate for the special needs of children of migrant workers. The President's "War on Poverty" program initiated efforts to change this situation at the federal government level. The Migrant Education Program was created by Congress in the mid-1960s as a result of the Elementary and Secondary School Act. For almost thirty years, it has provided essential instruction and support services for children of migrant farm workers whose education was interrupted or otherwise limited (National Commission on Migrant Education, 1992). The Improving America's Schools Act (IASA), signed by President Clinton in 1994, reauthorized the Migrant Education Program for the next five years.

For eligibility purposes, a migrant child/youth is one who moves across district lines for the purpose of seeking employment in agriculture or fishing. To qualify, the student must have moved within the preceding 36 months; prior to the 1994 IASA, students were eligible for six years. Funding flows from the federal government to the state agencies based on Full-Time Equivalents (FTEs). In turn, school districts can access funds through an application process. A total of $310 million for fiscal year 1995 and such sums as may be necessary for each of the four succeeding fiscal years were appropriated. In Texas, all school districts are required to identify and recruit migrant students even if they choose not to have a Migrant Education Program. Additional state funding may be available using Average Daily Attendance (ADA). If the district's enrollment is at least 5% migrant, the ADA may be calculated based on the best four reporting periods instead of all six reporting periods.

A variety of programs and intervention approaches have been implemented since the conceptualization of the Migrant Education Program. As migrant students and educators of migrant children, we have lived and experienced the different stages of implementation. The following is a chronological review of the evolution of the program based on personal experiences as migrant children and educators of migrant children.

Mid-1960s to Early 1970s: Segregated Classrooms

One of the early approaches in many Texas schools with high numbers of migrant students during the mid-1960s to early 1970s was to group all migrant children together. Migrant children were not only segregated through grouping, but in many cases were also physically detached from the rest of the school and excluded from activities. Finding and recruiting qualified and competent teachers to serve in this program was difficult. The children who needed the most help got the least experienced and less competent teachers. In many cases, migrant teaching positions were never filled, and uncertified substitute teachers were in and out of these classrooms year round. Supposedly, this model was implemented due to the categorical allocation of funds. This is a classic example of adapting the children's needs to fit the program instead of designing the program around the children's needs.

Early and Mid-1970s: Segregated, Six Months, Extended Day

During the early and mid-1970s, schools created a special calendar for migrant students congruent to their migration patterns. The school year was from November through April, and the school day was from 7:00 a.m. to 5:00 p.m. Since most migrant students had to ride the bus, it was almost as bad as going to work in the fields. A typical day was 12–14 hours long. Segregation seemed more defined. It had been hard for migrant students to participate in co-curricular activities before, but now it was almost impossible. They arrived at school before everyone else, ate lunch at different hours, went home after everyone else, and even rode different school buses.

Mid- and Late 1970s: Return to Segregated Classrooms

The compacted 6–month program did not last very long. Most schools returned to the initial segregated classroom model. This model was still in practice as late as 1976. One of us taught in this type of setting for three years. This approach had not been adequate or effective before, yet it was implemented again without any attempts to improve it based on the previous lessons of failure.

Late 1970s to Late 1980s: Integrated/Remedial Pullout Programs

It took over ten years for migrant students to be integrated back to the regular classrooms. Migrant students and migrant program teachers seemed reluctant to join the system that had long ignored them and kept them in isolation. Likewise, the system was not prepared to accept migrant students back into the mainstream classrooms. Though students were integrated, most were still grouped by ability and tracked. Schools set up remedial reading labs and pulled migrant students out of their classrooms for special instruction by resource teachers. The migrant label became even more negative and stigmatized for those students who were being pulled out. Everyone knew the negative criteria to go to the resource room. Only low-performing migrant students who needed remedial assistance qualified for these labs.

Early 1990s to Present: Pullout Accelerated Instruction

Some schools have genuinely shifted from remedial to accelerated instruction. However, many have just simply changed terminology and continue to serve the migrant students through ineffective and demeaning pullout remedial programs. A true accelerated instructional model can facilitate detracking for the migrant student population. All students receive the enriched curriculum generally reserved for gifted and talented students. The curriculum is not only fast paced and engaging, but also includes concepts, analyses, problem-solving, and interesting applications (Levin, 1987).

Present-Day Approaches: Schoolwide Projects

Currently, school districts with a high percentage of migrant students or students of low socioeconomic status are consolidating funds to serve all students in more heterogeneous settings. The IASA authorizes the combination of federal, state, and local funds for schoolwide programs that serve migrant children. This approach has advantages and disadvantages. One obvious advantage is that the categorical restrictions are lifted. All children have access to all programs, and they do not have to be stigmatized by labels. On the other hand, students who need the most services and generate the most funds may not access their equal share of these monies.

Purpose of the Migrant Education Program

As mandated by IASA 1994, the purpose of the Migrant Education Program is to assist states to:

1. Support high-quality and comprehensive educational programs for migratory children to help reduce the educational disruptions and other problems that result from repeated moves.
2. Ensure that migratory children are provided with appropriate educational services (including supportive services) that address their special needs in a coordinated and efficient manner.
3. Ensure that migratory children have the opportunity to meet the same challenging state content standards and challenging state student performance standards that all children are expected to meet.
4. Design programs to help migratory children overcome educational disruption, cultural and language barriers, social isolation, various health-related problems, and other factors that inhibit the ability of such children to do well in school, and to prepare such children to make a successful transition to postsecondary education or employmentand
5. Ensure that migratory children benefit from state and local systemic reforms (IASA, 1994, Sec. 1301).

The intent of the law is aligned to address the special needs of these invisible children of the road. The purpose is clear, but the results have not been very encouraging. We have been aware of the unique needs of migrant children for many years, yet after thirty years they still face many of the same conditions that have afflicted and hindered them throughout history.

Summary

In summary, migrant students face the same risks as many other disadvantaged students. However, it is evident that their unique conditions make them more intensely at risk than the general population. Among these conditions are high mobility, poverty, interrupted school attendance, inconsistent record keeping, limited English proficiency, and overage grade placement. The research clearly has indicated that educators who serve migrant children today are aware of their plight. However, for migrant children to succeed, educators must plan programs compatible with their affective, cognitive, and physical needs. Federal and state interventions in the form of mandates and funding have long been imposed on schools to assist migrant children. However, mandates are only as effective as the people who implement them. Many educators need to be clear about the purpose of mandates. Educators must see policies and mandates as a form of permission to be creative and not as a restrictive measure for inaction. While some improvement has been made, this population of migrant children continues to be one of the most at-risk and disadvantaged.

The few of us who have survived the system are indeed very fortunate. We have a wealth of experiences that help us see the world through many lenses. As children, these lenses were severely distorted by variables we had no power to control. As teachers, counselors, or administrators, we have significant power to influence the lives of the students we touch. No matter what group students belong to, they are the subordinates in schools; being different makes them doubly subordinate. It is extremely important that we understand and realize that being different is not necessarily inferior or a disadvantage. This awareness will help us also become cognizant of the similarities we all have as human beings. Most importantly, we must now move quickly beyond the awareness stage to a more inclusive stage of implementation and change.

Migrant children and those who live in poverty have special needs that must be addressed specifically. However, these children are also like all children. They have the same basic needs and they need to feel loved and be cared for. They also want to be treated fairly, with dignity and respect, and not made to feel inferior for their uniqueness.

III
THE STRUGGLES OF THE MIGRANT LIFESTYLE

⤙⤚

Introduction

This chapter chronicles life as migrant farm workers: how they survived, adapted quickly to challenge and change, and transformed their lives.

The following stories tell us about the lives of three migrant students: Belinda, Benito, and Sonia, who dared to turn around major adversities in their development and, beyond all expectations, succeeded in school. They learned to be highly flexible to adapt quickly to the changes in the different environments of the schools they each attended. Their success was not easy to achieve yet, they invested all the effort needed. They survived the hard work of the migrant lifestyle while going to school and were thus able to transform their lives. Our participants and their families told us about their family life and how the quality of their lives improved gradually as they became increasingly competent and successful in school— how education created options, opportunities, and choices. Though they knew that working the earth as migrant farm workers was honest work, they also knew that education would facilitate the process to break the cycle of poverty inherent in the migrant worker lifestyle.

What happens in the migrant families' lives, and how, even in extremely difficult circumstances, are they able to provide their children with what they need to succeed in school?

These migrant students traveled with their parents to work in the west and in the north, and carried with them the family hardships, burdens, and the heavy-duty work of adults, although they were young children emotionally, physically, and chronologically.

Nonetheless, as the family traveled the seemingly interminable rural farm-to-market roads and the endless field rows, they also carried their hopes, as they held intensely and dearly to their dreams of a better future for their children.

The family formed a circle of love that fortified the students when they thought there was no strength left. The children were their parents' joy, and working for their well-being made the parents happy. They believed in education for their children as a way out of the hardships they were experiencing, and they worked for what they believed in. It was neither a "free ride" nor predicated on a sense of entitlement. Nothing was free for them they earned their success.

Can you imagine for a moment what you may have seen behind their sun-darkened faces if you had been in the fields with them? Can you imagine the soulful eyes of those migrant mothers watching their children work hard until tears of pain and fatigue were rolling down their cheeks? If so, you may then be able to comprehend the depth of their compassion for their children's struggle, the endless strength emanating from their ideals and hopes, and the bittersweet beauty of a mothers' love.

The eyes of the migrant mother are the doorways to their hearts, the places where the love for their children resides. From their hearts, they give moral support and encouragement to their family and friends. In return they receive the joy of seeing their hopes for education and for a better future for their children become a tangible reality.

The beauty of the stories you are about to read is reflected in the effort, the struggle, and the joy of the migrant workers who found their hearts filled with the deepest satisfaction and the joy that came from seeing their beloved children attempting to reach the sky as they went to study at the university and came back home successful in their quest. Their vision of a better future for their children became a reality they now had a better life.

Belinda's Experience

The first year that Belinda remembers migrating was when she was in second grade. "One day my mom told me I wasn't going to go to school anymore. I was embarrassed to say that we were leaving school early to go work in the fields" (BM, 36–40). That day is vivid in her mind. Her mother went to pick her up early that day in May. "My teacher asked me in front of the whole class if I was going to school up there" (BM, 40–41).

Though her parents had been migrants before, this was the beginning of Belinda's migrant way of life. They left earlier than usual that year. Their first stop was in Uvalde, Texas. They picked onions and only earned enough money to continue their journey looking for work. They followed the crops to west Texas, where they chopped cotton. Most migrant farm workers refer to west Texas as *"El Wes."* They say, *"Vamos a los trabajos a El Wes* [let's go work in *El Wes*]." They went to Memphis, Odessa, La Mesa, Lubbock, Amarillo, Welch, and several other towns in west Texas. Belinda was confused.

> I didn't know it was west Texas, *yo no más oía vamos a El Wes a los trabajos"* [all I heard was let's go work in *El Wes*]. It was strange because to me that was not west Texas, it was more like north Texas. (BM, 45–47)

Belinda and her sister did not work that year because they were too young. They still went to the fields because they had nowhere else to stay. The first year she worked alongside her parents was in Memphis, Texas. *"Como quiera allí andábamos en la labor* [we were in the fields anyway] helping with the sacks, counting the *costales de cebolla* [onion sacks]." (BM, 11–14).

> I was only 9 years old. I had to be at least 12 years old to work. So my mom *me puso dos pantalones, y dos camisas, y los zapatos de mi hermano para verme más grande y alta* [She put on me two pairs of pants, two shirts, and my brother's shoes to look bigger and taller]. I needed to look older. I could see the boss outside [our house] filling out papers, and they called me. I felt strange because I was wearing all this clothing and I had to look really mature and older. I was only 9 years old. I remember walking out and standing at the door. The guy looked at me and started laughing. I don't know what he said or what happened after that, but my brother just told me that I was going to start working. *Dijo que estuvieras lista con el azadón* [He said you might be good with the hoe]. (BM, 87–101)

Belinda ran back in the house to tell her sister that she was going to work. She was excited and happy. The strategy had worked, but she knew they had not fooled the boss. "The *patrón* [boss] probably thought that I looked funny wearing all these clothes and I stood there trying to impress him so I could work. He knew I was not old enough" (BM, 107–109).

It was her mother's idea because Belinda had to be out in the fields anyway. The boss needed to approve her as an official worker so she could get paid. She and her sister did not really work as hard as the others. "We just walked around with the hoe and pretended to work, but we still had to be out there everyday" (BM, 109–111). They got paid the same ($2.25 an hour). Her parents helped them out as they followed them up and down the long rows of cotton. They did not care just as long as they got paid also. "That's why I needed to look old enough to work. It was now seven of us earning money. We went to *El Wes* until we were old enough to work by contract in Minnesota" (BM, 119–123).

As Belinda got older, she was expected to hold her own. Belinda did not like working in the fields, but she was a hard worker.

I'll never forget, I used to cry *de cansancio* (from fatigue). The thing that was real tiring was *el deshaije* (thinning). That was in Minnesota. It was constant and continuous, *azadoneé y azadoneé todo el día* [I hoed and hoed all day]. After a while your neck hurts a lot because you're just looking one way hoeing and hoeing. We did this all day long, 5:00 a.m. to 5:00 or 6:00 p.m. I cried and I thought, "Why me? Why me and not Dolly or Tracy?" These girls were rich kids that never worked in the fields. I wished it were they instead of me. I was in the sixth grade when this happened. (BM, 133–140)

Belinda and her family traveled to different places during the summers. They were migrant farm workers in west Texas, California, Wyoming, and Minnesota. Her parents waited as long as possible in the school year so their children would not have to miss any school. However, many times they had to pull their children out early because the crops were ready and the *patrón* needed them.

They went to California to work the grapes only a couple of years, and one year they went to Wyoming. Those were not productive trips because it rained a lot and they barely made enough money to come back home. As the children got older, Mr. and Mrs. Magallán decided to go where the children could help out. They always worked at *el azadón* (hoeing, chopping) because it was on a contract basis (by the acre), and all the family could help, regardless of their age. All of the Magallán children worked in the fields except Erica, the baby of the family. She was too young to work, but she was always out in the fields also. She stayed in the truck while they worked.

> My mom would buy her coloring books and she ate our tacos while all of us were working. That was pretty neat because all of us were together. That's about the only good thing about migrating. We were all together as a family. (BM, 475–478)

Belinda and her family started going to Minnesota in 1984 when they were all old enough to work by contract. They chopped beets for the same grower for 6 years until 1990. When Belinda became a sophomore, they decided not to go anymore.

In Minnesota they also did *"la piedra"* (the rock). "My mom *manejaba el tractorcito con una traila atrás y nosotros todos con un bote* [drove the tractor with a trailer and we all followed with a can]" (BM, 427–437). They picked stones and rocks in the fields. They got paid by the hour for this. The grower gave them this work because the beet fields were not ready yet. "Once we started working by contract, *no nos pagaban hasta que nos veníamos* [they would not pay us until we came back]" (BM, 438–440).

They tried to save all their money. "We never went out, never went to a movie, and we never bought anything. When we came back, we had all our earnings. *Veníamos ricos* [we came back rich]" (BM, 599–604).

All the Magallán children gave their earnings to their parents for the family budget. Their parents used some of the money to fix the house, but most of it they spent on their children. Belinda said her parents never bought anything for themselves.

> They would buy school clothes for all six of us. My dad would pay at the cash register, and I wanted to tell him not to spend it. It was so much work and he would just take out the bills and pay. All that hard work and in a minute you hand it to the clerk and it's gone. I would see her take it and I thought if she only knew how hard it was to earn that money. I remember *toda la ropa que nos compraban* [all the

clothes they bought us], the notebooks, colors, and the back packs. We always bought our things at K-Mart and Walmart. I thought those were great stores. I didn't know the difference until the fifth grade when kids started making fun. That year we didn't buy any clothes. My mom made it all for us. I remember the first day I was wearing yellow fluorescent pants with a white and yellow fluorescent shirt. A friend of mine asked where I had bought my clothes and I told her my mom had made it for me. She must have made me feel bad because that's the last year she made my clothes (BM, 608–622).

Mrs. Magallán seems to be the one who keeps track of their earnings. According to her, the last year they went to Minnesota they made some good money. They got paid $55.00 per acre for weeding and thinning beets. Each working member of the family made about $2,500.00. The grower did not pay them until the end of the summer when they had done all the work. If they needed money for food or emergencies, he would lend or advance them some money. Mr. Magallán did not mind this arrangement, because they were not tempted to spend their earnings before they came back to Texas. The grower offered them housing in a garage at no charge while they worked for him. The garage had been cleaned up, but did not have the amenities they had in their home back in Texas. They chose to live in the garage because they did not want to spend their money paying rent. They knew it was just a temporary situation and they could cope with it for a few months.

Housing was always substandard. Belinda remembers one house in particular. This was the house in *"El Wes."* It was in the middle of nowhere. They had to live there because there was nowhere else. Otherwise they would have to live in the car or under a tree or bridge. It was an abandoned house. The doors and windows were wide open, and the house was full of sand and dust. "My dad hosed it down, *le metió la manguera y lavo todo. Había arena en el piso* [he got the hose and washed everything. There was sand on the floor] and you could see the snake tracks all over" (BM, 633–641).

Belinda shared what is now a funny story. She was scared living in that old abandoned house.

Cuando me metía al [when I would get in the] shower I was scared to close my eyes so I wouldn't put any soap on my face. As time passed my Mom said, *"Hay mi hijita te estas poniendo morenita con el sol y te están saliendo pecas. Déjame ponerte aceite para que no se te pele la piel* [oh, my little daughter, you are getting burned by the sun and you are getting freckles. Let me put some oil so your skin won't peel]. (BM, 633–641)

Her mother wiped her face with a cotton ball soaked with lotion. *"Me limpió la cara y era pura mugre* [She cleaned my face and it was full of dirt]*"* (BM: 633–641). Her mother washed her dirty face. Belinda was sure something would crawl in and bite her if she closed her eyes while she showered. "This house had been abandoned for many years and *en la noche se oían muchos ruidos* [at night I heard a lot of noises]" (BM, 654–661)

It was a very big house and they used only half of it. That was the last time they stayed there. They never stayed in the same place twice except the last three years in Minnesota. The best place they ever lived in was in California. They had just opened a new labor camp for migrants that year. Everything was new. The mattresses were still wrapped in plastic, and these cabins had central air. They had indoor showers and restrooms. They were nice apartments. They did not stay there very long. They picked tomatoes, but they left for Minnesota because they were not making enough money.

Belinda dreaded every summer. She cried every time they left. No matter how many times they made the trip, it never got easier. As a young girl the only thing she liked about the trip was eating on the road. They never ate out in Rio Grande City, and it was a special treat to have a burger from a restaurant.

I would love those burgers. I never knew what a bought burger was until we migrated to go work. I remember one time in California. Isabel always ordered our food when we ate out because my parents didn't speak English. I remember he always got a "Happy Meal" for Erica, my little sister. When we left California, Isabel was not with us, but before we left I asked him, *"¿Cómo se llama esa cajita que le compras a Erica para encargársela yo* [what do you call that little box you get Erica so I can order it for her]?" He told me it was a "Happy Meal." When I ordered the first time they asked me what kind and I didn't know what to say. I was embarrassed because I thought I knew. Though I was the fifth oldest, I became the interpreter from then on. (BM, 655–668)

The most exciting part of the annual journey was the trip back. According to Belinda, coming home was the greatest feeling.

> The trip back was the most wonderful experience. Just driving back was so exciting. Driving into town no matter what time it was, it was great to be back home. It felt great sleeping in your own house, your own bed. (BM, 368–371)

It was great compared to sleeping on the floor. They never had beds anywhere except in California. The floor was hard and cold. All they had were blankets and sheets. No matter how good housing was over there, it was never better than their own house. Their home was always much more comfortable. It was a long three or four months while they waited for the day to come home. When the day would finally come it did not take the children long to pack. Belinda explained:

> We were packed and ready to go in 2 or 3 hours. *Ya vámonos* [let's go now]. My dad wanted to get a good night's sleep, but we wouldn't let him. All we wanted was to get on the road. He also wanted to stop and sleep on the road, but we convinced him to let Isabel drive while he slept. We wanted to get home quickly! *Cuando llegábamos a la casa, a veces llegábamos a la casa a las tres o cuatro de la mañana* [when we got to the house sometimes it was 3:00 or 4:00 in the morning], and we were wide awake. We got to the house, I took a deep breath, went to my room, and just laid on my bed because I couldn't go to sleep. (BM, 679–683)

Belinda's realization of the feelings of separation from their life in school, the loss of belonging to their school group, the realization of how unfair life is—giving some more struggle and others (such as rich kids) a life that appears easy—grew as she lived her dual life as a migrant worker and a school child.

Benito's Experience

Benito's migrant experience was short but intense. He was not in the migrant life cycle as long as Belinda or Sonia. However, as a young boy and "man of the family" he was expected to do a man's job many times.

We suspect it was more a self-imposed expectation. As with everything else, he worked alongside his mother and always tried to help her as much as he could. He and his mother worked in the fields every summer in Starr County. They picked melons, onions, peppers, and other crops. Benito's recollection of these experiences is scant:

> Well, basically the first times I remember I was maybe 6 or 7 years old when Mom used to work in the fields here. And I remember that we would go to La Casita Farms. Mom says that I used to help get her some melons and put them in the *costal* (sack). I remember those days because you know, the getting up early and Mom *hacía tacos de lonche* [made tacos for lunch]. And so, you know, that was the first recollection that I have of Mom working in the fields. (BG, 256–266)

Working in the fields so young made a big impression on Benito because he knew that most people who worked in the fields were uneducated. He believes he learned an important lesson. Benito is not ashamed of this, and is very proud of this experience. "Although it's very honorable work, I remember thinking that this was not the way I wanted to work the rest of my life, and I figured there had to be something easier than this" (BG, 275–278).

Benito and his mother became migrant farm workers when he was 11 years old. They traveled to Kansas several years and tried their luck in Washington one year. Not surprisingly, Benito does not have many pleasant memories of his migrant experience. He has mixed feelings about this ordeal. "Some of the worst memories I had were when we migrated, but at the same time they were some of the most telling experiences in the sense that they taught me something" (BG, 299–305).

Working in the fields was hard for a young boy like Benito. He talked about the long *surcos* (furrows) in Kansas that were miles long. It took hours to get from one end to the other. Benito felt overwhelmed.

> I was expected to do a man's job. It's sort of tough not to cry when you are 13 or 14 years old. You are expected to do that, and everybody else is pretty much older. That was in Kansas. (BG, 323–326)

The first year that Benito went to Kansas he could not work in the fields because he was only about 11 or 12 years old. However, the owner of the ranch hired him as his personal helper. It was a way to give him work without violating the child labor laws. Benito got up early every morning with his mother. The crew leader picked them up and drove them to the fields with all the other workers.

> Robert would come and pick me up in the fields. I would drive around with Robert all day and then the whole day I would either be laying pipe with him, or he would take me to the house to clean the combines. I would have to get inside the machines and clean them out. I would also do things around the house for them. Of course, I was getting paid for doing this. Then in the *tardes* [afternoons], by the time everybody was getting ready to finish in the fields, he would go leave me with everybody and I'd just come home. (BG, 336–339)

He did this only the first year. The next few years he worked in the fields with all the other workers even though he was still underage. Mrs. García said that Benito hid in the furrows when inspectors came to the fields, much the same way many others hid from border patrol officers. Benito said,

> Yeah, because that was when . . . in those days they started to get into these child labor laws a little bit more intensely. You know, there was a lot of that going on. I remember that in Kansas, I was always on the lookout to make sure I saw the truck before they saw me so I could hide. (BG, 468–477)

Benito and his mother went to Kansas for three years. They went to Washington when he was in the eighth grade. It was the same thing or worse there. Benito remembers this year well because it was the only year he dropped out of school early to go work. He has distinct memories:

> I remember because I didn't go to the eighth-grade prom, and I didn't go to the graduation ceremony. My Mom has always felt pretty bad about that. That year we left, like, in March. All my friends talk about the eighth-grade prom, so I guess it must have been better than our senior prom. But Mom has always felt bad that I didn't graduate from junior high. (BM, 749–756)

They went to Toppenish, Washington, to pick asparagus and stayed to pick cherries in the Mabton area. Cutting and picking asparagus is one of the most backbreaking jobs migrant farm workers do. As a 13–year-old, he cried in the fields many times.

> We were always the last ones to get the tractor, my Mom and I. And Mom couldn't bend down. So I would end up picking *el espárrago* [the asparagus] by myself. By that time, everybody was already gone to the camp and *allá andaba yo solo* [there I was by myself]. (BM, 758–784)

Benito drove the tractor himself. By the time he and his mother were ready to load the boxes, no one else was there to help him load them on the truck.

> I would have to load them by myself, and some of these weighed 30 or 40 pounds. I mean, it's not a lot except it is hard when you have to load 30, or 40, or 50 all by yourself all the way to the top. Those were very difficult experiences where I cried. (BG, 490–493)

As young as he was, Benito knew he and his mother needed to do it. He said they would actually save a couple of hundred dollars by the time they went back to Texas. Benito said that was more than they could ever earn here. He appreciates the wisdom he gained from these difficult experiences, but does not wish them on anyone else.

> Those experiences taught me a couple of things. Number 1: the difficulty of what it is to be a minor in an adult world of work. Number 2: that most kids don't ever have the experience of being expected to do a man's job when they are 12 or 13, and yet most migrant children go through this. These children do not have a choice, they have to do the job. It's understandable that you can't do it exactly like a grown man, but you are expected. You pretty much have to suck it up. But by the same token, if you can withstand something like that and live through it, you learn to appreciate the little things in life better. (BG, 524–536)

Benito and his mother did not go back to Washington, but made one more trip to Kansas when he was a freshman. From then on he worked at school with the summer programs while his mother continued to pick melons in local farms. He also worked for Mr. Salinas at the local funeral home during the school year until he graduated. Benito thinks highly of Mr. Salinas. Mr. Salinas helped Benito unselfishly when he was in need.

Benito was one of very few migrant students whose housing conditions were better in the labor camps. Housing conditions could not possibly be any worse than his own home in Texas. In Kansas, the rancher provided a farmhouse for all his workers. It was a big house with six bedrooms and a kitchen. Though each family had their own bedroom, they all shared the kitchen and the bathroom. Everybody got up and rushed to the kitchen to make their lunches for the day. The same was the case for the bathroom. Benito felt bad for his mother.

> My Mom, *pobrecita* (poor Mom), she was always the last one to be given the kitchen. You know? We had to go through those things because she was a widow and, you know, some families had some *mal modos* (bad manners) and they were mean. So she would be the last one to make *el lonche* (lunch). And then, of course, the crew boss would charge us . . . $10.00 a day just to take us to the fields. (BG: 544–557)

In Washington they lived in labor camps. They were like apartments, each with its own kitchen and bathroom. Compared to living conditions in Texas, Benito said,

> At that point, I guess, in a way they were better than ours, in my view, than my house anyway. We had a shower over there. There was a restroom. So to me, they were better for that reason. But I guess if, for other migrant kids they'd probably think it was worse than being home, but I don't know. (BG, 570–577)

For Benito and his mother, it was significantly better; it was a drastic improvement. However, being away from home was never easy. No matter how many more amenities they enjoyed, there was nothing like going back to the warmth of their own home.

Benito's experience left him with the feeling that, in comparison with the hard, honest life of a migrant worker, laboring at school was relatively easy.

Sonia's Experience

Sonia knew the routine well. She described the annual ritual. All it took was a phone call from Mr. Ramírez's brother (the crew leader) in Washington, and the preparations for the trip began.

Sonia and her family left Texas in late March or early April to pick asparagus in eastern Washington (Connell). When the asparagus season was over in late June, they moved on to northwest Washington to pick berries. When we were there in 1996, they got to Lynden on June 28. In early August, they made one more stop to pick cucumbers in the Mt. Vernon area. When this last project was done in late August, they went back to Texas and started all over again. In October, the children stayed in Texas, while Mr. and Mrs. Ramírez went to Oregon to work in the potato fields.

For about six months, they traveled together, worked together, lived in very tight quarters together, and took care of each other. For the last twenty-one years, since they came to this country, this lifestyle has given them the opportunity to spend quality time together. There was a strong sense of family unity, which is almost expected living in a communal setting like this.

The children made the necessary arrangements to withdraw from school and everyone helped with the packing. The family made one final trip home to México to say goodbye and secure the home they owned there.

> Well, usually we did all the packing the night before. So, in the morning, we just had to get up, get ready, and get in the truck. Everything was packed already, and the food was bought the night before. All the clothes were packed like the week before. (SR, 799–806)

Once they had taken care of all these matters, they were ready for their journey to Washington. "I remember my dad always liked to leave early in the morning. So we were up at about 4:00 and left at about 5:00 in the morning" (SR, 799–806).

Their yearly trek took them through what is called *la ruta de los migrantes,* the migrant's route, for those going to Washington. After many years of traveling, migrant families had figured this route to be the shortest and fastest. They left the Rio Grande Valley and entered New

Mexico through El Paso, Texas. In Gallup, New Mexico, they went north on *la 666* (Highway 666) through Cortez, Colorado, and west to Utah. The drive through Utah took them to Moab and on to Salt Lake City. Idaho came next, followed by Oregon, before they reached their first place of work in southeastern Washington. The drive is beautiful. We have driven this route several times ourselves. However, when migrant families were on the road, their main objective was to get to their destinations safely and as soon as possible. *"Lo que queremos es llegar, no tenemos tiempo para apreciar y disfrutar el camino* [All we want is to get there, we do not have time to appreciate or enjoy the trip]*"* (FR, 22–24). It took about forty hours to drive approximately 2,500 miles. It was not a fun trip, according to Ana (Sonia's sister). Her father was not the type that liked to enjoy the scenery. He wanted to get there as soon as possible. "We would just stop maybe at a rest area just to stretch our legs and so forth, and get something to eat, then just head on." According to Sonia,

> At night, I remember that he didn't sleep very much 'cause we were asleep by the time he stopped, and then when we got up he was still driving. So we didn't even know if he had stopped to sleep or not. I know that part of it was because he wanted to get us there safe. (SR, 843–850)

The drive to Sunset (Washington) labor camp was about 20 miles from Bellingham, and 6 miles from Lynden. Outside the city was a completely different world—the world of agriculture. After exiting Interstate 5, the country roads were surrounded by lush vegetation and farming. While there were still many tall trees separating one field from another, most of the area was farmland. Lynden was about 100 miles north of Seattle and about 50 miles south of Vancouver, British Columbia. There were many fields, and they all looked alike. There were strawberry, blueberry, and raspberry fields all over, and some vineyards. Texas migrant families, generation after generation, had been picking berries and working in the canneries in this area.

Many families used public phones at convenience stores. People were standing in line waiting their turns for the phone. Most people called their relatives back home once a week, on Saturdays or Sundays. The growers live in nice homes with neatly manicured lawns. The camps were nowhere to be seen. It was uncertain if the camps or the beautiful homes were the anomaly in this area. Perhaps the camps were hidden away so they would not steal away from the beauty of these homes.

Like many other migrant labor camps, this camp was well hidden, out of sight, and, in a way, invisible. The fields were secluded behind lines of trees, and people not paying attention never really saw the migrant workers in the fields. However, they were evident in the grocery stores, laundromats, and many other businesses in the area. They spent thousands of dollars in the community and surely contributed to the economy much the same way winter visitors ("snowbirds") contribute to the economy of the Rio Grande Valley. They picked the crops and also helped consume them.

Sunset labor camp was one of the nicer camps we had seen. On one particular Saturday, it seemed more crowded than usual. Everyone was out washing their clothes and hanging them on the clotheslines to dry. Children were playing and several of the men were just hanging around talking. Because it was the weekend, all the children were home. The camp was full of life.

In Connell (eastern Washington), Sonia's family lived in a small labor camp. According to Mr. Ramírez, "*Había cuatro o cinco trailitas en este campo y nosotros vivíamos en una de ellas* [There were four or five little trailer homes, and we lived in one of them]" (FR, 77–79). Sonia said the mobile home they lived in was not too bad. It had three bedrooms, a kitchen, and, best of all, indoor plumbing. "It doesn't feel very good at the beginning, but we have more room and privacy here than in the other camps. Every time we move, it gets worse" (SR, 402–404).

In Lynden they lived at the Sunset labor camp. This camp has over 60 units or cabins. The grower requires that there be a minimum of eight workers in each unit. Sonia's family had only five working hands, but no one complained.

There were three long buildings that looked like barracks constructed of bright silver corrugated aluminum sheets. Each cabin was no larger than 30 square feet. There was no closet or storage space, and all of the family's clothes were either in boxes or on the beds. Needless to say, they were extremely crowded, with little room for anything other than sleeping, cooking, and eating. It would have been extremely crowded had there been the eight required working hands living there.

It was admirable how Sonia and her family were always nicely groomed and neatly dressed. They had a sink (no hot water) to wash dishes, a stove, a picnic table, and a refrigerator. The cabin was also furnished with three full-size bunk beds and an old couch another family left behind. They had community showers and toilet facilities in another building located in the center of the camp. Sonia said it was inconvenient not to have facilities indoors.

> It is hard during the night if you have to go to the restroom. I need a flashlight to get there. Hot water is also a problem. If you are not one of the first ones to shower, you either take a cold shower, wait until the morning, or skip it. It gets cold up here in the evenings. The camp manager lives in the camp and they are the only ones to have indoor plumbing. (SR, 414–423)

Housing got progressively worse every time they moved. When they moved to Mt. Vernon to pick cucumbers, they were forced to live in dreadful conditions. "It gets harder and harder, but we know it's getting close to going home so we just keep going" (SR, 426–428).

There were about fifteen units in this camp. The cabin was a shack much smaller than the one at Sunset camp.

> It's really small, it's just like two small rooms. One is the kitchen, and the other one's the bedroom. All the bunks are in one so we're all crowded. All five of us, and we're all crowded in one room. We try to make like a little corner for the pillows and stuff. And then the kitchen is probably the biggest room, but still it's really small 'cause what doesn't fit in the room has to fit in the kitchen. The toilets and showers were bad. There were three showers and three outhouses for the whole camp. (SR, 867–876)

Sonia and her family were really glad when the work at Mt. Vernon was over. They quickly packed their belongings and started their trip back to Texas. They had a very nice and comfortable home in Texas with all the amenities they could never imagine having in the labor camps in Washington. It was admirable the manner in which they adapted to the living conditions they were exposed to as migrant farm workers. Mr. Ramírez said they endured it because *"sabemos que es no más por un rato* [we know it's only for a short while]" (FR, 87–89). However, to them *"un rato"* (a short while) was almost half the year.

They did not have a mortgage to pay because they paid as they built it piecemeal. When we asked Sonia's father if they owed any money on their home, he answered with pride, *"No señor, no debemos nada, todo está pagado* [No sir, we do not owe anything, everything is paid for]" (FR, 88–89). Like many other homes in the Rio Grande Valley, it was a cinder-block home, a white stucco house with red composition roofing and a two-car garage. Sonia showed us her house which was very spacious. It was a large four bedroom home with two bathrooms, a washroom, and an open dining and kitchen area. We sat in the living room, an attractive room with tile floors and wood-paneled walls decked with pictures of the children and their parents. Sonia was in México with her parents the first time we went to visit, and Cristóbal and Rey were home by themselves. It felt and looked quite different the next time we visited when their mother was there. The house was noticeably cleaner, organized, and there was a sense of warmth in the air.

We drove around the neighborhood. It seemed like a neighborhood where many migrant families lived. There were cars with license plates from all over the U.S. (Nebraska, South and North Dakota, Indiana, Wyoming, Minnesota, Washington, Oregon, Utah, California). There were also many cars with Mexican license plates.

Last year, Sonia and her family got to Connell, Washington, in early April. They moved into their mobile home in the camp and started working as soon as they settled in. They picked asparagus for one of the major canning companies. Picking asparagus is the hardest work they do. Mr. Ramírez said, *"Es muy duro este trabajo . . . te mata la cintura* [This is a hard job . . . it kills your back]" (FR, 103–105).

For the work they did, they felt they did not make enough money. Each family or group was assigned to pick a set number of acres from a particular field everyday. Since asparagus spears grow from one day to the next, it was not uncommon for a family to pick from the same piece of land the whole season. When the family was through with its acreage, they quit for the day. They were paid 14¢ a pound. On a good day, the family could pick from 1,500 to 1,800 pounds. However, sometimes as many as 500 pounds were deducted by the time the asparagus was separated into quality categories. Thus, as a family of five they earned about $175.00 for 10 to 12 hours of work each day. This translated to a little over $3.00 an hour per person. They do not like it, but they have been doing it for 21 years. *"Es la necesidad de trabajar, ya estamos impuestos*

[It's the need to work, we are used to it]," said Sonia's mother (AR, 149–151).

They picked asparagus for three long months, day in and day out. In late June they made their way to Lynden to pick berries. Most of the workers in Lynden in early July were picking strawberries. Others had begun to work in the cannery because they had also started to pick raspberries, which are used for juice and jam. As the strawberry season came to an end in late July, the raspberry season began. Raspberries were mostly picked by machines, except when they were needed fresh for market. Though these machines were displacing hand labor, the labor camps were still full and crowded. As we drove to the camp, we saw several machines picking even though it was raining. They did not stop picking unless it rained hard and they could not move in the mud. Each machine required at least three people to operate it. They needed a driver and two others in the back cleaning out debris as the berries were carried on a conveyor belt into baskets. These machines were tall, and looked like giant insects straddling the berry plants as they moved along each row shaking the berries off the plants.

A typical workday started at about 4:00 a.m. Sonia's mother got up earlier to make their lunch, which was usually flour tortilla tacos filled with *papas con huevo* (potato and egg), beans, or just plain eggs. They ate when they got hungry, since they worked by weight, not time. They were at the field by 5:00 a.m. and immediately started picking. They put in an 8- to 10-hour day, depending on how fast they combed the fields. They filled their buckets and weighed in when they had filled at least four of them.

Strawberries were still picked by hand and workers were paid 13¢ a pound. According to Cristóbal and Sonia, a good picker could pick about 750 pounds a day. Cristóbal said he could pick about 450 pounds on a good day, while Sonia said she can pick about 150. During peak season, the family picked about 2500 pounds per day and made about $325.00. This was almost twice as much as picking asparagus. Sonia does not like to pick strawberries. It is hard stoop labor. "It is very hard work and it does not bring enough money, but I like it better than picking asparagus" (SR, 887–888).

We looked at her young hands as she was talking to us and noticed they were stained purple from the berries. Almost everyone in the camp had purple hands during strawberry season, and no matter how much they washed, it would not go away. It looked like a contagious skin disease contracted by everyone in the camp.

This year the strawberries were late and the workers picked for about three weeks. When the strawberries slowed down, Sonia's father, mother, and Cristóbal began work on the raspberry machines. Here they got paid by the hour, depending on what they were assigned to do. Drivers could earn up to $6.25 an hour, while the cleaners earned slightly less. Sonia and Rey continued picking strawberries until there were none to pick. Not all the family worked on the machines because the grower tried to spread this work around so all families could continue to work.

We asked Mr. Ramírez, "How much longer do you plan to do this?" He answered, *"No sabemos, quizá un año o quizá diez, ¿quién sabe?* [We don't know. We may do it one year, we may do it 10, who knows?] " (FR: 123–125).

It would get harder and harder to get housing at the camps because they would not have enough working hands in their family to merit the space. Sonia's parents continued to go north to pick crops, but as their children graduated and went to college, they were no longer expected to make the trip. They were gradually working themselves out of a job by promoting their children's success. As the living conditions worsened because the size of the family (in terms of numbers of workers) diminished, the family remained committed to the goal of betterment of the children's lives. The family continued to absorb the hardship, which was the cost of that goal.

IV
THE FAMILY—SUPPORT AND INFLUENCE

⊸

IN THEIR FAMILIES, THESE MIGRANT FARM WORKER CHILDREN LEARNED GUID-
ing values, beliefs, and hopes for the future. They also learned to trust:
to trust oneself, to trust others, and to trust their ability to reach a better
future. They might have been poor by economic standards, but the effect
of the loving family diminished the impact of difficulties and increased
their feelings of self-worth and self-confidence.

Their families gave them the love they needed to develop solid self-
esteem and self-confidence. They learned to cooperate for the common
good of the family. Just as the light of hope showed them the path that
led to a better future, they also learned the power of unity: All for one
and one for all.

The vision of a better future encouraged them to give all they had and
to go beyond their limits in order to complete their work and to do it
the best way they could. They shared their effort and even sacrificed for
the other family members. They helped each other and kept on going.

Belinda's Biographical Data

Belinda is an intelligent, highly motivated, and very determined young
woman. At 22 years old, she has lived a life full of experiences that have
helped her mature into a very assertive, confident, and responsible person.
She is quiet, but very articulate. She is respectful of others, but expects the
same in return. She is willing to work hard and determined to be successful.

Belinda is the fifth child of a family of six, and the second of three girls. She was born in La Casita, Texas, on May 18, 1975. This was just five days after her parents came to the United States legally. She was born at home, and delivered by a neighbor who happened to be a *partera* (midwife).

Mr. and Mrs. Magallán spoke of their daughter with great pride. They both said Belinda has always been a hard worker at home, at work, and especially at school. No matter how tired she was, Belinda hardly complained when they were out in the fields. During the summers, she worked long hours in the hot sun or cold mornings alongside her parents. Since her parents do not speak English, their children have always had to interpret for them. Though Belinda was the fifth child, she assumed the role of interpreter when she was about 12 years old. Mr. Magallán explained,

Belinda no tenía verguenza hablar con los patrones Americanos . . . tenía mucha confianza en si misma y era como una abogada para nosotros [She was not shy when she spoke to the boss . . . she was self-confident and she was like a lawyer for us]. (MM, 23–24)

As she interpreted for her father, she also successfully negotiated their wages most of the time. Belinda was always very assertive and the *patrones* respected and admired her even at that young age, explained her mother. "*Desde que yo me acuerdo, Belinda siempre ha tenido mucha ambición y empeño con sus estudios y con su trabajo* [Ever since I remember, Belinda has always had ambition and dedication with her studies]" (MM, 34–35).

She has always had extraordinary energy. Her mother said, as a young child, "*ella todo el tiempo me ayudaba con el quehacer de la casa* [she always helped me with the housework] (MM: 37–39). She would clean the house, sweep, mop, wash clothes, and cook. "*Yo no me mortificaba de nada, ella tenía la comida lista para todos todo el tiempo* [I did not have to worry about anything, she always had dinner ready for everyone]" (MM, 42–44). This gave Mrs. Magallán more time to sew. When Belinda was home, Mrs. Magallan said, "*Yo podía coser hasta tres vestidos en un día* [I could sew up to three dresses in one day]" (MM: 46–48).

Though Belinda is so assertive and proactive, her mother says that Belinda "*todo el tiempo ha sido muy noble* [has always been very noble]" (MM: 48–49). She is a caring person who would never hurt anyone.

"*Trata a la gente con mucho respeto* [She always treats people with respect]" (MM: 54–58).

We went to visit Belinda's parents to begin gathering data in December of 1996. We had trouble finding their house because we could not make sense of the way streets were planned out. We did not see any street signs anywhere. This *colonia* (neighborhood) was in what is called La Santa Cruz, a small community about 5 miles east of Rio Grande City. Most people who lived in Belinda's neighborhood are or were migrant farm workers. The majority are recent immigrants from México. The architecture of these homes made this evident. Most homes had flat roofs, cinder-block walls, and wrought-iron windows, doors, and gates. Most homes were painted bright green, blue, red, pink, or yellow. The original part of Belinda's house was a frame home constructed by a local lumber company. As the family grew, they added rooms using traditional concrete and cinder block. It is a fairly large three-bedroom home on a spacious lot. Their lawn is shaded by several large trees. A satellite dish sticks out on the front corner of the house. The house is painted a bright aqua green color. It is now too big, since all the children have moved except Belinda's youngest sister.

We finally found her house after driving around a few times. They were not expecting us, but Belinda had told her parents about our study. Only Belinda's mother and her youngest sister were home. Mrs. Magallán was busy, but she dropped everything to talk to us. We explained what we were doing and what our study was about. She was very interested and willing to help in any way they could. She was very happy that Belinda was part of the study. We made an appointment to come back so we could also speak to Belinda's father.

The next time we came to visit them was very productive. We sat down on the couch, and took out our notebooks and pens. Time seemed to fly and before we knew it, we had been there an hour and we had not taken any notes at all. We asked a few questions and that was enough to generate a lengthy discussion. It was as if they knew exactly what we wanted to know. They talked about their personal backgrounds, where they were born, and where they grew up. They also told us about some of their experiences as they traveled to different states as migrants to do agricultural work before and after becoming legal residents.

Mrs. Magallán was more articulate than Mr. Magallán. She was more specific and explained things in detail. Mr. Magallán was more general, but very insightful. He seemed more patient, and she seemed more energetic. Mrs. Magallán appeared to be the more proactive one of the two. They were very nice and cooperative. They felt it would be a great experience for Belinda, and they were willing to do anything they could to help.

Jesús I. Magallán is Belinda's father. Belinda looks very much like him. He was born in México on a ranch named Santa Gertrudis on November 27, 1945. He was 51 years old at the time of the interview, and is the youngest of five children. This ranch is just a few miles across the river from Rio Grande City on the Texas/México border. He went to school in México, but only finished *primaria* (sixth grade). According to him, he always won *"los primeros lugares"* (first places) in his class. He has worked in the fields almost all his life. At 12 years old, after he left school, he went to work in his father's *parcelas* (fields). The cash crop was corn.

Belinda's mother is Marta López Magallán. She was also born in México on a ranch named Los Villarreales close to Mr. Magallán's birthplace. Mrs. Magallán was born on August 2, 1947 and was 49 years old at the time of the interview. She was very articulate, had an extensive vocabulary, and expressed herself clearly. She was the youngest of five children and the only girl. According to her, she and her parents lived comfortably in México because they owned some land, which her father farmed. She never worked in the fields until she immigrated to the United States in search of a "better life." She never imagined she would travel throughout the United States as a migrant farm worker. Her father did not allow her to work in the fields when she was growing up. Like her husband, she and all her brothers also went to school only through *primaria* (sixth grade). After she finished sixth grade, she stayed at home and helped her mother with the daily housework. Her dream was to be a schoolteacher, and she wanted to continue going to school. Unfortunately, her father did not let her because the closest *secundaria* (secondary school) was in Camargo, about 25 miles away. She knew that her father would never have let her go simply because she was a girl. According to him, said Mrs. Magallán, *"Las mujeres no necesitan educación porque se van a casar con alguien que las mantenga* [Women do not need an education because they are going to get married with someone who will take care of them]" (MM, 3–8).

Mr. and Mrs. Magallán got married in 1966. She was 19 years old and he was 20. Their romance started when Mr. Magallán gave Mrs.

Magallán and several of her girlfriends a ride in his 1952 Chevy truck. This was the same truck he used to haul corn and other crops. She and her friends were going to *el cine* (theater) on a Sunday afternoon, and Mr. Magallán happened to drive by as they were waiting for the bus on the side of the highway. She was one of the lucky ones to crowd into the cab and sat next to Mr. Magallán. They looked at each other and soon started the *noviazgo* (courtship). By 1996, they had been married for 31 years.

They have seven children. Jesús I. Jr., Isabel, José Armando, Dora, Belinda, and Erica. Jesús and Isabel were born in México. Though the family did not legally immigrate until 1975, Juan Alberto was born in the United States. Mrs. Magallán explained that she wanted her son to be born in the United States in order to facilitate their efforts to gain legal entry. The oldest of the girls, Dora, was born in California on their first trip as migrant farm workers. Belinda was the only one born in Rio Grande City, Texas. Erica, *la coyotita* (the baby), was born in Memphis, Texas, on one of their trips. Four of the first five children graduated from high school. One dropped out, but eventually earned his diploma through the GED program. Jesús and Dora earned associate degrees in refrigeration and nursing, respectively. Juan is a certified welder, and Isabel is a travel agent with a major airline. Erica was an eighth-grade honor student.

Mr. and Mrs. Magallán and their family came legally to the United States on May 13, 1975, the same day they got their *micas* (documents). They came across the border through the Rio Grande City, Texas, port of entry. Their first home was in the small community of La Casita, about 10 miles east of Rio Grande City. They lived there from 1975 to 1983, when they moved to their present home. Mr. Magallán gained employment with one of the largest growers in the Rio Grande Valley. He held permanent employment with this company until recently, when he got laid off because of the drought. Throughout these years, Mr. Magallán explained, he worked out an arrangement with his boss that allowed him to do migrant farm work during the summers. When he returned early in the fall, his job was waiting. This was an opportunity to make a little more money because his wife and children could also work. Once they came back to Texas, Mr. Magallán was again the only wage earner. Mrs. Magallán also held a few jobs, but never on a regular basis. As a seamstress, she helped supplement their earnings by sewing at home. At the time of our study, they were living on unemployment benefits, which were about to run out. Some of their older children were helping them financially to pay their bills. Mr. and Mrs. Magallán are very proud of all their children.

Mr. and Mrs. Magallán were very protective of their girls. Belinda could not even imagine asking her parents if a boyfriend could come visit. No boys ever came to her house even when she went to the prom. "I had to meet my date for the prom at a local burger stand. There I was with a formal dress and he with his tuxedo. I didn't want anybody to see me. I felt so dumb" (BM, 267–271). She wanted to ask her father, but her mother told her, "*No le preguntes a tu papá, ya sabes lo que te va a decir* [Don't even ask, you know what he's going to say]" (BM, 273–277). Belinda could not make any sense of it because he knew she was going to the prom. "I never dated anyone from my own high school. I dated boys I met at dances or other places" (BM, 281–283). Consequently, she said she never had anyone walk her to class or carry her books. She never got a mum for homecoming, or a Valentine's card, or helium balloons. "I remember seeing those girls with those huge mums hanging all over the place. That's one thing I've always thought about, when I have my own daughters I'm going to send them the mums myself" (BM, 345–350).

She arranged to work from 5:00 p.m. to 12:00 midnight on weekdays so she could have Saturday evenings off to socialize. Her mother never knew it was her choice. "I worked from 5:00 to 12:00 midnight, then I came home to study and do my homework" (BM, 365–367). When she took this job, she stopped riding the bus. Her mother drove her to school so she could sleep a little longer. "The bus would pick us up at 6:30 a.m., so I would sleep longer if she took me" (BM, 369–371).

Her parents were the same or harder with her older sister. Her boyfriend did not come to the house until he asked for her hand in marriage. It was different with Belinda. Maybe it was because she was the second daughter. "My father met my boyfriend at my sister's wedding. He even asked to meet him and then invited him to the house for the party after the reception. It was quite a surprise to me" (BM, 438–441).

Mr. Magallán was still very protective. When Belinda came home to visit from college, she invited her boyfriend, but they had to drive in separate cars. Her father did not want them riding in the same car, so her boyfriend followed her home in his car. "I drove straight home and he checked into a hotel. It was not until college graduation night that we drove in the same car together. I didn't ask, I just did it" (BM, 401–404). She knew her father did not like it, but he did not say anything. Belinda was the center of the family, and held the family together. Everything revolved around her. She assumed a role usually assigned to the oldest son or daughter. Her parents and siblings depended on her for guidance and assistance.

Belinda is totally committed to her parents. She is very intuitive and sensitive. She told us her mother had surgery but pretended to be fine. Belinda said she knew her mother was in pain. She had been in pain for a while, and her husband had to force her to go see the doctor.

Belinda was also concerned about her father's employment status. In November of 1995, Mr. Magallán went on sick leave from his job. He procrastinated going to the doctor because he thought he just had the flu. His breathing became more difficult, and his coughing spells got worse. Mr. Magallán had been exposed to pesticides and insecticides for years. He developed a kind of hard lining or coating in his lungs from this exposure, according to the doctor who treated him. In May of 1996, the doctor told him he could return to work. According to Belinda, he returned to his job, but his hours were cut drastically. After about a month, he was laid off because the company was closing down the Starr County site because of the drought. Belinda was sure his poor health was the real reason for his layoff. She felt they could have offered him a job in one of the other sites operated by this company. Belinda was resentful because her father served them for many years. She was angry and frustrated. "That is the life of the farm worker. We are exploited until we are worn down and then cast aside like a machine that becomes obsolete and too expensive to maintain" (BM, 140–146). Belinda could sense the frustration her father was experiencing because he had never been unemployed in his life. His unemployment benefits were about to expire. She felt sorry and sad for her father. He had been looking for agricultural work everyday with no luck.

I keep telling him to try other kinds of work, but he does not want to because he says he cannot speak English. And I tell him, *y para qué necesita hablar inglés, aquí todos hablan español* [and why do you need to speak English if everyone speaks Spanish here]. (BM, 148–150)

We commented that it was admirable the way her brothers were help-ing while her father was unemployed. Her semblance changed quickly. Belinda was honest and to the point. She wanted to set the record straight about her brothers. She told us her oldest brother had been in jail. Jesús had been caught selling drugs, spent 2½ years in prison, and was now living in San Antonio. She also told us that Juan (third oldest brother) had been severely addicted to drugs. We were quite surprised to hear this, because her parents had not said anything about this. Juan was now sober but still struggling financially. Belinda thought it ironic that one brother sold the drugs and the other consumed them. Belinda shared this simply to let us know that these two brothers had never helped. On the contrary, she explained, "My brothers have been more of a financial and emotional burden for my parents" (BM, 35–37).

Her other brother, Jesús, was doing well and helps, but he kept his distance. Belinda was disappointed, hurt, and angry. She had to help her parents out although she was a full-time student and working part time. She signed a lease for her oldest brother's apartment in San Antonio and had to lend him money for the deposit. The other brother calls her collect when he needs to talk to her.

Mr. and Mrs. Magallán wanted their children out of the migrant life cycle. They tried to support their children the best way they could. Unlike many other migrant families, they always returned to Texas before the first day of school in the fall. They could have stayed longer and earned a few more dollars, but they returned because "*lo primero eran los niños, no queríamos que faltaran la escuela* [first it was the children, we did not want them to miss school]" (JM, 59–63). Belinda's parents always made sure they came back to Texas early. "My parents made sure we were back by the first day of school. Even if there was still work we would always come back. Other families would stay and go to other states also" (BM: 101–106).

Her parents cared, but they could not conceptualize what Belinda wanted. She wanted more than just going to "a college." They were proud that she had graduated from high school, but they would be satisfied if she just went to a technical school. Her brothers and sisters had done that, and they had decent jobs. Belinda had higher aspirations, and she did not know why it was so hard for her parents to understand. They valued education and encouraged their children, but Belinda won-dered why her parents did not expect and demand more.

Your parents are supposed to be the ones who push you to do more. My parents would ask me why couldn't I be like my sister. They wanted me to go to a technical school and stay close to home. They asked: "Why are you breaking your head? Why are you studying so hard staying after school? Just go to regular classes." I was afraid to speak up. I didn't know what to tell my parents. I didn't want to hurt their feeling or show disrespect. When I met you and Mr. G. [García], I learned that it didn't have to be that way. Really, I think I owe it to you two. (BM, 215–222)

Benito's Biographical Data

Benito García is the oldest of the three participants in this study. He represents those who have made it through the public school system and college, and are professionally successful. Benito was one of several candidates that met the criteria for participation in this study. His story was most inspiring and seemed almost fictional. It was an unbelievable journey full of challenging obstacles and exciting experiences. Benito was very easy to talk with, and he was a very good listener. He was also articulate. He loved to talk and share his experiences.

Benito was 36 years old. He was born May 26, 1961, at La Puerta Ranch in Starr County, Texas. It is a small community about 5 miles east of Rio Grande City, Texas. He is about 5'10" tall, heavyset, and weighs about 235 pounds. He has a very light complexion, dark brown hair, and brown eyes. He is the only child from his mother's second marriage, but he has two half-sisters and a half-brother. He is married to Araceli B. García, and they have two children, Benito Jr. (age 8) and Oscar Omar (age 4).

Benito has lived in Rio Grande City all his life. It is located in Starr County, part of the Rio Grande Valley in deep south Texas along the Texas-México border. According to the U.S. Census (1990), Starr County was the second poorest county in the nation. The data showed that 74.21% of the population was below the poverty line ($6,451) compared to 20.05% for the state. The population of Starr County is about 45,000. Rio Grande City, the county seat, has a population of about 10,000 people. Demographically, it is almost 100% Hispanic, with a few Anglos and almost no African Americans. The economy of this area depends mostly on farming and ranching. The major employers are the school district and the county government.

We interviewed Mrs. García, Benito's mother. It was difficult to open the gate to her home, so we climbed over a barbed-wire fence to get to the house. We knocked on the door, and Benito's mother greeted us. We felt welcomed and comfortable as she invited us into her home. It was cold that day, and space heaters warmed the house. Her oldest daughter, Lucía, had come from California to spend a few weeks with her after learning of her mother's cancer diagnosis. We sat at the kitchen table and explained the purpose of our visit. Mrs. García was interested and willing to help us out as much as she could. "*Yo estoy para ayudarte con lo que pueda* [I am here to help you with whatever I can]" (NG, 2–4).

Benito's mother's name is Norma García. She was in her seventies, but looked fairly strong. She spoke softly but eloquently and powerfully. She radiated pride and self-confidence. She spoke with great pride of her son. Her story is just as moving as his.

She was born and raised on a ranch known as Las Letras, close to the small town of Puruándiro in the state of Michoacán in central México. Her parents, like most people in this community, depended on agriculture for a living. It was barely enough for subsistence. Mrs. García had no formal schooling. She has learned to read some on her own, but writes little. She married, had three children, and was widowed young. Life was extremely hard for Mrs. García and her children.

Widowed and desperate, Mrs. García and a friend came to the United States in search of a better life in 1954. It was perhaps the hardest decision she ever had to make. She left her two daughters and son with her parents and boarded a bus to the Texas-México border. She and her friend crossed the river somewhere between Camargo, Tamaulipas, and Rio Grande City, Texas. Mrs. García did not imagine she would ever return to live in México again. With the help of a *coyote* (smuggler), whom they paid $10.00, they swam across the river during the night and hid in the thicket overnight as they waited for someone to come get them. "*Nos escondimos en un arroyo toda la noche y teníamos mucho frío porque la ropa nunca se nos secó* [We hid in a creek all night, and we were very cold because our clothes never dried]" (NG, 2–4).

Her friend had been to the United States before and knew some people for whom they could work. Someone finally picked them up in the morning and took them to a small ranch east of Rio Grande City known as El Refugio. They stayed there for a day or so before she was taken to what would become her home for the rest of her life. She immediately went to work for Lorenzo and María Barrios at El Brazil Ranch. Her primary responsibility was to care for María's elderly father. She was paid about 50 cents a day for her work. "*Me pagaban $16.00 por quincena* [They paid me $16.00 every 2 weeks]" (NG, 2–4).

While working for this family, she met and married María's brother, Adan García. She continued to care for the elderly man who had suddenly become her father-in-law. Her husband worked at a local brick factory where Lorenzo Barrios (brother-in-law) was the foreman. Thus, Benito's parents both worked for the Barrios family.

Benito's father was given a few acres of land by his elderly father and they continued to live on El Brazil Ranch after they married. "*El primer año que nos casamos no teníamos nada. No teníamos ni vasijas para cocinar* [The first year we were married, we had nothing. We did not even have dishes for cooking]" (NG, 6–7). The second year they were married, they went to work in Lubbock. They became migrant farm workers and traveled to west Texas to supplement their meager wages. "*Nos fue muy bien porque compramos las cosas necesarias para vivir* [It went very well because we were able to buy the things we needed to live]" (NG, 14–15). They were also able to buy their first and only car. They paid $150.00 for the 1949 Dodge sedan that still sits next to Benito's childhood home. When they came back, Benito's father began to build what became their home for the next twenty-two years.

Mrs. García talked to us about how much her husband loved his son.

Se pasaba todo el tiempo que podía con él. Todo el tiempo se lo llevaba con él al trabajo. Empacaba las cosas del niño y lo envolvía cuidadosamente en sus cobijitas cuando aún estaba dormido y lo echaba al carro todas las mañanas [He spent as much time as possible with him. He always took Benito with him to work. He would pack up the baby's things, wrap him up carefully while he was still asleep, and put him in the car every morning]. (NG, 27–30)

While his father worked, Benito stayed with his aunt close to the factory. Though Benito was only 3 years old when his father passed away, he remembers driving home from work and stopping at a gasoline station where his father would often buy him Frito corn chips.

Tragedy struck again for Mrs. García. Her husband suffered a deadly stroke and passed away at the age of 47. After only six years of marriage, she was again a widow. This was the beginning of a life totally dedicated to raising her son. "*Nos quedamos solitos nada más él y yo sin nadie quien nos ayudara* [We were all alone, just my son and I, with no one to help us]" (NG, 44–48). Suddenly, she was alone and away from home with her 3–year-old son. She had no family or relatives other than her in-laws, but they offered little assistance or support. It was as if they also had died.

The first time we visited with Benito he told us that his mother had been diagnosed with cancer. He was emotional and tried to hold back his tears. He was completely preoccupied with her condition.

When her husband passed away, Benito and his mother became one. She gave every living moment of her life to her son. All they had was each other, and together they began their struggle through a long and difficult journey. Their main source of income was a $40.00 monthly social security check and food stamps. When he turned 18, his mother no longer received any benefits, but Benito began to draw a monthly social security check because he was in college. Immediately after he received the check, he endorsed it and sent it to his mother. To supplement their income, she worked in the fields and at other odd jobs whenever she could. She took good care of her son. Though they were extremely poor, he was always well clothed and never went hungry. "*Yo le cosía su ropita, hasta sus calzoncillos le remendaba* [I would sew his little clothes, and even mend his underwear]" (NG, 112–114, 56–60).

No matter what kind of work she had to do, she was always home when her son came home. She always had dinner ready for him when he came home from school. "*Le gustaban mucho las papas y todavía le gustan* [He liked potatoes very much and he still likes them]" (NG, 112–114). She showed us a bag of potatoes she had bought especially for him for when he visits. "*Siempre viene a verme y le hago de comer. Le hago sus taquitos para que se lleve* [He always comes to see me and I cook for him. I make him tacos so he can take some with him]" (NG, 112–114, 80–85).

Benito explained his remarkable relationship with his mother:

It just never ends. She is just embedded in everything that happens and that I do. All my life when I was growing up, it was just she and I. I knew everything she was doing, and she knew everything I was doing. I always knew where she was. You know, to this day when we are in the same building or same house, sometimes out of instinct I still tell her, "*Voy para el baño, ma, ahorita vengo* [I'm going to the restroom, Mom; I'll be right back]." I usually . . . like when I was going to school, I never left without Mom giving me her kiss, and coming home, the same thing. And it's something that Sally [wife] and I share. And something that the kids and I share. Maybe because that was the way I was brought up. And I think, you know, it's a little different when you are raised as an only child. I guess, you know, you come from a larger family. It's a little different for Mom to give more attention to one particular child than the other. Well, she gave everything to me. I didn't have to fight over the last slice of toast, or the last piece of chicken. It was always there for me. And . . . I think, you know, when talking to some of my friends, I can sense the bond between me and my Mom is different than all my friends with their moms. It's stronger, it's different, and not because it's better, but simply because it was a different type of sacrifice, a different type of bond that's between us. (BG, 33–58)

As a 36–year-old married man, Benito still maintained an incredible relationship with his mother. He feels the relationship and commitment is stronger than ever. He continues to practice the rituals that helped them survive alone and together.

I usually don't leave town without her knowing where I'm going. Sometimes it's hard. Sometimes I have to call her from the airport or as soon as I get over there. But almost for sure . . . no matter where I've traveled all over the country, I usually don't go to sleep before Mom knows where I'm at. It might be from the airplane, or from the airport, or from the other airport, or from my cab or something. You know, and she comes to expect it from me, and I just don't feel good not doing it. (BG: 47–58)

Mrs. García made many sacrifices for her son, and Benito was aware of that at a very young age. He shared a moving story that exemplifies what his mother meant and means to him.

In our house there were never really gifts. Never had a party, I didn't have my first birthday party until Sally sort of had one for me. I remember this particular Christmas. I was going to be 6 years old. And that Christmas, I remember waking up and there in the living room at the house was a banana bike, with the old banana seat. And I remember feeling like—man! This was the greatest gift of all time. And it meant a lot because I knew then, and more now, number one, she couldn't afford it. And she later told me now as an adult that it took her I don't know how many months to pay that thing off at the Firestone. You know? It was like 40 or 50 bucks then. And I remember feeling—boy! It's just the greatest gift that I've ever received. And when I look at the feeling, I've never had that feeling, never again. Not like that. Not getting the college degree, not getting a law degree, not becoming married . . . that feeling has never been equaled. Maybe because every time you get a reward, before you get that reward there's sacrifice, there's work, there's a lot of things. But it's sort of like, it's sort of like the story in the Bible where, you know, all the men are giving their coins and this little old lady goes and gives two coins and Jesús *le dice* [tells her] that she's going to be more blessed because unlike the others that are giving *lo que les sobra* [what they have left over] in their pocket, this old widow gives everything she's got. And it makes a big difference if a person gives everything she's got as opposed to *lo que le sobra* [what they have left over]. And maybe that's why. And—well, the bike was just a bike. I've had brand new cars. I have a swimming pool. I know what it is to make a lot of money. I've owned a Rolex. And a tailor-made suit. But nothing has ever, ever felt as good as that particular gift. I was 6 years old. I'll never forget it . . . never forget that. I think if there was one experience that means more than anything to me it's probably that one because I think that epitomizes what my Mom means to me. (BG, 64–101)

His close friends knew where he lived yet they never thought of him as being poor. Gerardo, one of his childhood friends, said that maybe it was because he "never heard him complain or use it as an excuse. No matter what, he always tried hard and never used it as an excuse. He was determined, dedicated, and driven. I knew he would make it because he has lots of heart" (GG, 5–7).

However, Benito knew he was different from his friends. He was aware that he was poor compared to them. At a very young age Benito knew that everything his mother did for him was a major sacrifice.

Oh, yeah. I mean, I used to get a quarter a week. You know, as an allowance. But I could see, even when I was a little older, you know, Billy and Roland, they used to get a dollar a day. That was a lot for me, but I never felt that we were poor in the sense that we needed something because we were poor. As a kid I remember I didn't have fancy clothes but I was always clean, I was always ironed, dinner was always done when I got home, I always got breakfast before I left for school. (BG, 159–172)

El Brazil Ranch is about 8 miles north of Rio Grande City. The countryside is beautiful in its own way. The rolling hills are similar to central Texas, but the vegetation is very different. It is brush country with mesquite being the largest trees. An old, crudely made sign that reads "El Brazil Ranch" is the only marker along the barbed-wire fence that lines the road. About a mile down the bumpy and dusty dirt road lies a group of houses. Benito's house is the last home at the end of the road.

There was an interesting sign on the gate with his name. When he played football in high school, it was a practice for varsity players to put up signs in their front yard with the number of the football player that lived in the house. Benito's weathered sign was still up. However, he had slightly modified it by overlapping one of his political campaign signs over the old football sign. It now reads, "Benito García for Mayor [new sign] lives here [old sign]."

When we entered the small structure that had been Benito's home for the last twenty years, it was inconceivable that anyone could live in such substandard housing and survive. Benito's father started to build this house before he passed away. It is a small, wood-frame shack that sits on piers and is no bigger than about 12 by 20 feet. It is still covered with the same gray, simulated-brick, composition siding. Inside, it is divided into two small rooms. One of these is the kitchen. His mother did not have a stove and cooked over coals until Benito bought her a gas range when he was in college.

The other room is a combination living room and bedroom. Half walls divide these two areas. On the side next to the kitchen was a full-size bed.

I shared the same bed with my mother because I did not want to hurt her feelings by sleeping on the couch. On the other hand, I also worried that my friends would find out. *Me daba vergüenza que mis amigos se dieran cuenta* [I was ashamed that my friends would ever find out]. (BG, 80–85)

On the other side was the living room, which was scantily furnished with a sofa and other pieces of furniture. Outside was brush country at its best. The mesquite trees, buffalo grass, and the weeds were all brown at this time of the year. The only green vegetation were the large cacti native to this area.

On the backside of the house lay his father's old rusted 1949 Dodge on its side. Benito said, "*Allí es donde está el carro* [That's where the car is] . . . my dad's car is where he left it when he died in 1964." On the same side was the outhouse Benito and his mother used for a long time. They never had indoor plumbing. They did not have a shower or indoor restroom. During the winter it was very cold in the house. His mother warmed water over a fire so he could take a bath.

No matter how poor we were, I was always clean. I remember I was still in bed when my mom would iron my clothes so they would be warm when I put them on. My clothes were worn out but clean and pressed all the time. (BG, 112–115)

In sharp contrast, next to Benito's childhood home sits their newer home. It is a wood-frame house Benito built for his mother when he was a junior in college through an FHA loan. It is a few times bigger than their old house. It is a one-bedroom home, but Benito added an extra bedroom when he moved back to Rio Grande City to practice law. It is equipped with amenities such as indoor plumbing, a gas stove, and air conditioning. The walls are decked with Benito's pictures, awards, and mementos. Benito lives in his mother's home even when he is not there physically.

Benito wanted to do away with the old house after they built the new one, but his mother convinced him to keep it for sentimental reasons. Benito is glad she did not let him tear it down. Not long ago, a family asked Mrs. García if she would rent it. Benito did not want to rent it because it was not in any condition for anyone to live in. The family was homeless and his mother convinced him to let them stay there because they had nowhere else to go. "*El no quería porque la casita estaba en malas condiciones* [He did not want to because it was in bad condition]" (NG, 102–106). Benito helped them fix it up, and the family still lives there rent free. He also pays for their utilities. His mother is proud of him. "*Mi hijo es muy bueno . . . si puede ayudarte, el te va ayudar de una manera u otra* [My son is a kind person . . . if he can help you, he will help you, one way or another]" (NG, 112–114).

Sonia's Biographical Data

Sonia was in the migrant life cycle since the day she was born.

> My brothers told me that they were all asleep the night I was born, and when they woke up in the morning, nobody was there. And they were scared . . . well, they were crying and stuff 'cause they were still small. They were wondering what had happened. And then the next thing they knew, my Dad came with food, and told them that they had a new sister. All my brothers and sisters had stayed alone while I was being born. David was the oldest and he was only 7 or 8 years old. (SR, 7–17)

The five children, ranging in ages from 2 to 8 years old, had no idea where their parents were. That night, David and Ana found themselves taking care of their younger brothers, not really knowing why they were alone, how long they would be alone, or if their parents would return.

Sonia knew that her parents expected them to do well in school. She said, "My parents have given me a lot of encouragement. They value education a lot" (SR: 251–263).

Sonia is a mature, resilient young woman who at a young age has already overcome tremendous obstacles to survive and succeed. Her story is indeed an amazing journey through a life full of challenges. Sonia has been in the migrant life cycle since the day she was born. She was born in Toppenish, Washington, on October 10, 1978, during one of her family's trips to work.

Sonia is about 5' 3", medium build, with dark brown hair and big, beautiful brown eyes. Her face and skin color are a beautiful creamy brown. (In Spanish, we call this skin color *aperlada* [pearl-colored].) She is shy around people she does not know well and does not say much unless prompted. She said, "I've always been quiet. Shy." (SR: 379)

We learned from Mr. Ríos, one of her teachers, that she suffers from juvenile rheumatoid arthritis, and yet, "she never complains, she always does her work and everything else that needs to get done. She has lots of ambition, a great attitude, and is definitely hardworking. She is very shy but articulate when she needs to be" (Mr. R, 25).

When we talked to Sonia's father, Franco Ramírez, and her mother, Amalia, about the study, we explained that it was going to require some of their time and intrusion on their privacy. They were willing and ready to allow their daughter to participate. Mr. Ramírez assured us it was not a problem for them.

No es ninguna molestia para nosotros, aquí estamos para ayudarle como puedamos y es una buena oportunidad y experiencia para Sonia [It is not a bother for us, we are here to help however we can and it is a good opportunity and experience for her]. (FR, 27–30)

The Ramírez family came to the United States in 1974. Making a living in México was hard, and raising a family was even more difficult. A bad drought wiped out the crops and forced Mr. Ramírez to sell his cows and goats before he lost them all. "*También trabajábamos las tierras, pero se vino una sequía y se nos puso muy difícil* [We also worked the lands, but we had a bad drought, and it became very difficult]" (FR, 59–62). With the help of his brother who was already in the United States, he used this money to cover the expenses required to gain legal entry for his family into this country.

Mr. Ramírez was 54 years old at the time of our study; he was born on May 11, 1943, in Los Ramones, Nuevo León, México. Los Ramones is a small community about 50 miles south of the border between Monterrey and Reynosa. He was very courteous and accommodating. He spoke softly but convincingly. He is very proud of his family. All their children have graduated from high school. He seemed to be the one in charge of checking up on the children's schoolwork and report cards. According to Mrs. Ramírez,

El se encargaba de ayudarles con las tareas y revisar las calificaciones. El se sentaba con ellos y les ayudaba, les ayudaba mucho [He was in charge of helping them with their school work and checking their report cards. He would sit with them and help them, he helped them a lot]. (AR, 15–18)

Though he spoke and wrote minimal English, he always tried to help them with their schoolwork.

Mr. Ramírez was also the disciplinarian. Sonia's sister, Ana, said that her father was understanding, but had high expectations for all his children. He always demanded their best at school and in the fields. He was firm but flexible. He was compassionate, but accepted no excuses. Mr. Ramírez went to school in México when he could. He came to the United States with his parents when he was young, and worked in Arizona and Oregon. He went to school but did not stay long.

Iba a la escuela en ratos no más; fui unos dos o tres años. Todo el tiempo me ponían con niños más chicos que yo. Tenía trece o catorce años y me ponían en segundo o tercer grado. No cabía en los pupitres [I went to school only sometimes; I went maybe 2 or 3 years. They always put me with children younger than me. I was 13 or 14 years old and I was placed in second or third grade. I did not fit in the desks]. (FR: 52–57)

He went back to live in México when he was 18 years old.

Mrs. Ramírez was 51 years old. She was born on a ranch known as El Porvenir in México. She finished *primaria* (sixth grade) in México. She is the oldest of nine girls and two boys. Her parents made a living running a mobile store selling goods from ranch to ranch. She leaves the schooling and discipline matters to her husband. However, she is in charge of the family finances and budget. Though Mr. Ramírez is in charge of most family functions, his wife knows more about the finances and budget. She is the one who knows how much money they earned last year.

They have six children, David (27), Ana (26), José (25), Cristóbal (21), Rey (19), and Sonia (18). The three oldest were born in México. David earned his associate's degree in electronics. Ana graduated from St. Edward's University and is now a teacher in Austin, Texas. José is currently enrolled at The University of Texas, Pan American. Cristóbal and Rey graduated from high school and are still working with their parents. Sonia is now enrolled in St. Edward's University.

Though Sonia's parents have earned an honest living and are proud of what they have accomplished, they do not want their children working in the fields for the rest of their lives. Both parents always encouraged their children to go to school. Mrs. Ramírez said,

Bueno, pues, nosotros no queríamos que fueran como uno. Uno quería que los hijos fueran más arriba, y que estudiaran. Queríamos que fueran a la escuela. Es una vida muy dura y es duro para uno ver que sus hijos sigan trabajando en la labor. Nos venimos a los Estados Unidos para darles una vida mejor a nuestros hijos [Well, we did not want them to be like us. We wanted them to do better and to study. We wanted them to go to school. It is a hard life and it is hard for us to see our children working in the fields. We came to the United States to provide a better life for our children]. (AR, 67–74)

That had been their hope and expectation for all their children. Consequently, Sonia had known for a long time that she was not going to be a migrant farm worker forever. According to Sonia, her parents

always encouraged and urged us to do our best in school. My parents have helped me a lot. They've taught me that education is the only way for me to get along with my life, and I'll be able to support myself. And not have anybody support me. My parents have given me a lot of encouragement. They value education a lot. . . .They tell us stories about their troubles when growing up that . . . when they were younger they didn't have . . . well, they hardly had food. (SR, 251–263, 98–115)

Sonia's parents had a unique and subtle approach to encourage their children to succeed: They did not demand perfection from them, but they expected their best efforts. They did not preach hard work, but they modeled it. They did not set goals for them, but they set the standards. Her parents were an inspiration to her, and the driving force in her life.

Everything Mr. and Mrs. Ramírez did revolved around their children. There was a strong sense of support and security. Sonia shared a seemingly insignificant but powerful anecdote with us during one of our interviews.

My dad . . . well, my parents, both of them, they always put us first. Our education. Everything. Their children go first before them. When we were working in the fields, I was missing one of those rain gears, and my Mom loaned me hers so that I wouldn't get wet. She had another one. But it was kind of torn. So, she got it. She gave me the new one. And she got the torn one. And well, they've always done that. Always put us first, or try to help us first, they are very support-

66

ive. Well, they've always been there for us. They've tried to help us whenever we've needed them. And they're nice. They're loving. They're caring. If my parents wouldn't care about education, I don't think I would have done as well. They're always telling us that that's the only way that we can live well . . . and stuff, that we all need an education, all the time. It doesn't matter what you study, just as long as you get something together, a stable job. (SR, 98–115)

She also knows that the reason she and her siblings have done fairly well is because of the family unity and the support for one another her parents have facilitated and nurtured. As the youngest in her family, she has enjoyed the attention naturally given to the baby of the family.

I was kind of spoiled 'cause I was the baby, but only when I was smaller. Yeah, my sister and my brothers all of them helped me. What we've all gone through is the same. So we all, we all tell each other that we have to . . . that we have to finish school. That we have to keep going and keep studying. And, well, since I'm the youngest, everybody tells me. I get talked to a lot. (SR, 157–155)

While the three oldest got more help from their parents with their schoolwork, Sonia got more help from her older brothers and her sister. Her parents were not actively involved in school, but they attended school functions regularly. Sonia knew her parents expected good grades.

My father always checked our report cards to make sure we had good grades. They expected us to try our best. To do our best . . . if you had a C or whatever, they would ask us why and they would understand. Like they wouldn't go right away and say you just didn't try. They'd, like, ask if we tried our best. (SR, 167–173)

Sonia's sister, Ana, simply said, "There was just really no question in my mind that I was going to finish high school and go to college. It was understood, there was no compromise" (AR, 135–130). Ana felt that her parents were stricter with the first three children than the younger ones.

I think my parents were very strict with David, myself, and José because they had just gotten into this new country, and they wanted to make sure that we succeeded. And they were very strict with us. Homework, school, you know, good grades. If we got a bad report card, they would really get after us. (AM, 32–38)

Ana always got good grades, but she remembered that David and José got punished for getting bad grades once in a while. "I think with Cristóbal, Rey, and Sonia (the youngest), they were a little bit more laid back" (AR, 45–47).

Nevertheless, she says, her parents never gave up on Cristóbal and Rey. They still graduated from high school because they were very smart. Sonia learned from these experiences. She had Ana as a role model on one side and on the other, she witnessed her younger brothers' struggle and the anguish it caused her parents. Consequently, she did not want to disappoint her parents. "But, mostly I want to do it for myself 'cause I want to further my education" (SR, 64–66).

Sonia's parents feel she will do well in college because she likes school.

Todo el tiempo fue muy dedicada a sus estudios. Le gustaba mucho escribir y leer desde que estaba muy chica. Nosotros nunca tuvimos que decirle que hiciera sus tareas [She has always been dedicated to her studies. She liked to write and read since she was very little. We never had to tell her to do her homework]. (AR, 123–126)

They do not want Sonia to go far away to college, but they are ready to support her decision. "*Nosotros estamos dispuestos a apoyarla para que siga estudiando y logre sus propósitos* [We are willing to support her so she can achieve her goals]" (AR, 144–145).

The guiding force of Sonia's success (and that of other migrant children), the parental and sibling setting and modeling of high standards, provided the migrant children with the tools needed to accomplish the goals that their parents had set.

The migrant familys' legacy to their children's success was manifold— but that legacy appeared to be grounded in the familys' power to influence the personal development of the students as independent, proud, persistent, and courageous human beings. The students were armed with the dreams of their parents, the empowerment occasioned by their parents' sacrifices, and the abundance of love and support of a strong extended family. Thus armed, they were equipped with self-esteem, confidence, and inner power for success.

V

THE SCHOOL

⊸

School Work Versus Field Work: Mental Versus Physical

The school of life for migrant students was hard. Life was not fair—and yet, life's unfairness could bring out the best in them. Anybody could survive, and beyond that, anyone could thrive. In their hearts, they hoped for a better future. They were taught to give their best effort and even to sacrifice for the others. The migrant students in our stories were able to convert misfortune into good work and gain strength from adversity. The experiences in the fields led them to have stability in times of uncertainty and turmoil. It led them to develop a conscious self-concept of professionalism and to do their job the best they could. The hard work they went through in the fields took so much effort and sacrifice that they now expect tough situations to work out well for themselves and for others.

Belinda's School Life and Experiences

Children had all kinds of labels and Belinda seemed to have them all. She was migrant, immigrant, economically disadvantaged, at-risk, female, and Hispanic. Though her ability was questioned and her feelings were hurt, she refused to believe that she was not capable. She took it as a challenge, and she was more determined to prove them wrong.

Belinda stood out in the crowd. She was tall and lanky with a full head of long curly hair that seemed too big for her small face. She looked awkward, but she also projected a strong sense of self-confidence and presence.

Belinda was an excellent student, and she remembered doing well in elementary school. She attended Guerrero Elementary from Head Start through the fourth grade. Head Start is her most memorable year because her mother won the attendance award for PTA meetings. Her memories about Head Start were clear.

> I remember my mother taking me to Head Start the first day. That's the only year I remember my mom attending PTA meetings. My teacher, Ms. Pérez, had a chart on the wall with the names of our parents. She would put a star each time parents went to a PTA meeting and my mom had the most stars on the chart. She won the attendance award for my class. My mom was very involved that year, and my dad was usually at work. He would come pick us up. I don't know how my mom got to the meetings. The meetings were after school so I would just stay there instead of going home on the bus, and I would leave with my mom afterwards. (BM, 23–30)

Belinda did not remember the name of her kindergarten teacher, but she said it was fun, and she enjoyed going to school. The only thing she remembered about kindergarten was that someone took her to the store and bought her a jacket for winter. Belinda even remembered the name of the store.

> They would take us to Antonio's. It was just the migrant kids that went. That year my little neighbor, Bertha, and I both got jackets. I didn't like the jacket my teacher had chosen for me. I liked Bertha's and she liked mine so we traded. It was a reversible jacket. It was green and red. On one side it was green with white polka dots, and on the other, it was red with white polka dots. (BM, 89–97)

Nobody told the migrant students why they got the jackets, but everyone else knew why. The teacher would read the names off a list, and they would tell them they were going to the store to get their jackets. Belinda was aware that other children knew why she and other students were getting jackets.

I didn't feel too good because there were some kids that made fun of us. They knew it was the poor kids getting the jackets. We knew we were the poor kids, and it was like they wanted us to know that. (BM, 114–118)

By first grade it was clear to Belinda that students were grouped by language, and the English-speaking children were considered the "smart kids" in the school. She wanted to be in the "smart class" with Ms. Reyes. She was labeled LEP (limited English proficient) and was placed in the bilingual classroom with Ms. Boras.

I always wanted to be in Ms. Reyes's class. She was the one that used to like turtles . . . she had them all over the room. I always wanted to be in her class because that's where the smart kids were. I knew that only because that's what our teacher would tell us. Even our own teacher would tell us they were the smart class. (BM, 121–125)

Her parents never requested or asked for a particular teacher the way other parents did. Some parents demanded certain teachers for their children, and their demands were usually honored. Belinda's parents never knew they had choices. They were not aware of the politics and the practices. They did not know that everything was negotiable if they advocated for their children actively. Those who knew the system got the best of it.

Belinda said, "In first grade, I remember getting lots of awards. I was there for the awards assembly at the end of the year. I got awards for honor roll, perfect attendance, and for the highest scores in a health competition" (BM, 128–132).

The first day of school was always full of anticipation. She was anxious to see who her teacher was going to be. Without fail, this anxiety always turned into disappointment. Her biggest hope was to be placed in the "smart" class, but her name was always on the other list. She kept hoping to be in the more challenging classrooms. Her pain was evident as she spoke of her experience.

In second grade I was embarrassed because I was placed with the bilingual kids. The teacher would make me read Spanish, and I didn't want to. I wanted to be in the other class with the smart students, the ones who spoke English. I was embarrassed to tell you the truth. Everyone thought that we were the dumb ones. In all these early grades there was always the class for Spanish speakers and the one for English speakers. It was the dumb class and the smart class. I could see that the smart class was the kids of the high class. The ones that were always well dressed, the ones who had the nice satchels and huge boxes of crayons. I was aware at that young age. It doesn't make sense now; the kids that needed the most help always seemed to get the worst teachers. (BM, 138–146)

Belinda then went to Redfield Elementary because it was the only school in town that housed fifth graders. Consequently, there were many more students and the competition to get the "best" teachers was more intense. Belinda found herself again in the same kind of classrooms she had always dreaded.

Oh, I remember my fifth grade teacher, Mr. Guerra, at Redfield Elementary. One time he was very mad at us. We used to have our class upstairs. Downstairs was the GT [gifted and talented] teacher, Mr. Dayna. He told us when he was really mad that if we would be smart we would be downstairs with the smart kids, not up there with him. There were a few of us who turned out to be successful. We were not seen as smart because all the smart kids were in the GT class downstairs with that teacher. (BM, 150–159)

After one year at Redfield Elementary, she went to Redfield Intermediate (a school with sixth grade only). Sixth grade had been part of the junior high school, but it was a new campus when Belinda became a sixth grader. As a sixth grader she continued to do well, but she was still unchallenged. The only thing she remembers about sixth grade is that everyone made her English teacher cry. She wanted to be in the band that year, but her parents did not let her because they did not want her to stay after school. That meant they would have to come get her after practice, and they could not do it everyday. Her brother was in the band, but he had to quit for that reason. She tried to convince her parents to let her join the band.

We still had my brother's cornet. I took it to the band director and he told me he could get me in. When I told my mom she told me I couldn't join. I also wanted to play sports, but that also required staying after school. (BM, 162–164)

Then she went to junior high, and seventh grade was not much different. In a matter of four years she had been to four different campuses. As a seventh grader she was not in athletics or in the band. Her standardized test scores kept her from qualifying for the gifted and talented program. This was a disadvantage for Belinda and many others because the majority of gifted and talented students automatically qualified for the more "prestigious" classes. This track was considered more rigorous and challenging, and the students were aware of it. The expectations were higher for these students. The more popular classes and teachers were always full by the time the migrant students enrolled. Nevertheless, Belinda found a way into this track in the eighth grade.

This was the year she finally broke out of the stronghold the system had on her. It was indeed the turning point in her life, but it was also a painful experience. Year after year, she left before the school year was over, and never had the opportunity to participate in extra curricular activities. Her eighth-grade year was different. Mr. G. encouraged her to try out for the impromptu speaking team. Belinda accepted the challenge and made the team. She had never competed or won anything. Belinda worked hard and won the district championship. According to Mr. G., she had a lot of self-discipline and determination. Her words are still clear in his mind: "Sir, I'm going to win the district championship. I don't care how long we have to practice. I don't care what we have to do, sir. I want to win" (RG, 240–243).

So they practiced weekends, nights, mornings, and lunch time. Mr. G. said she never let down. That took a lot of self-discipline and a lot of commitment for a 14-year-old.

She wasn't originally on the first team, but she would hang around. I was coaching other students, which would always rank higher than her. Belinda would come in third or fourth all the time. And suddenly, when it came down to the nitty gritty, she won it all. (RG, 54–60)

Suddenly, Belinda was popular and acknowledged by her teachers and peers. She began to be noticed. The principal selected her as the main speaker for the promotion ceremony. She was honored, and she could hardly wait to tell her parents. Her parents shocked her back to reality when they told her they were leaving to go work in Minnesota again. She was angry and resentful for being the daughter of migrant farm workers. She could not understand why her parents would not postpone their departure. The principal offered to pay for her airfare if her parents would let her stay with a relative until school was out. She knew her parents would never allow it, but she still asked only to be disappointed again. Just when she was beginning to feel good about herself, she was abruptly reminded that school life and success were not congruent with her way of life. It was a big let down for Belinda, but she transformed this seemingly traumatic episode into another life-inspiring experience.

Belinda's particular experience helped us (her middle school educators at the time) realize that migrant students led a life no one fully knew nor understood. We were also convinced that no one could tell this life story better than the student herself. Mr. G. therefore decided to get a group of migrant children together and asked them to write their stories. They worked for months and produced scripts that combined their experiences into five mini-dramas to share their stories. Belinda began to tell her story. She was one of fourteen migrant students who participated in presentations at the state and national migrant conferences in the fall of 1989 and spring of 1990. The students had to be current migrants in order to participate. Mr. G. reminded us that

> these were all students who nobody knew. They had never participated in anything. As far as I know, not a single one of those kids was what we call popular. They were unknowns, they were nobodies. Of course, they were somebody to us. They were our kids. Nobody recognized them or gave them the time of day. They were undiscovered. Once they became discovered, suddenly everybody wanted them in their classes. People wanted to talk to them. The Rotary Club invited them to lunch and stuff like that. (RG, 62–70)

These children mesmerized the audience with their stories and their talent. The participants found themselves on an emotional roller coaster—screaming with laughter then struggling in vain to hold back tears. They confronted the audience boldly with issues and strong emotions. The students' dramatic sketches pulled no punches. They were inspired by true incidents from the lives of the participants.

Belinda's participation in impromptu speaking was a training ground for these migrant conference presentations. She was extraordinarily articulate and dramatic. It was evident that she took pride in her involvement. Belinda said,

> It was such a good experience telling other people my story . . . telling them what I had gone through. Some of those teachers that saw the presentation thought that just because I was migrant or I was leaving early I couldn't do just as well as anybody else. Just because I was migrant I was placed in the regular classes. It didn't have to be that way. (BM, 247–253)

When Belinda went to high school, most people knew who she was because of these presentations. All the teachers in the district got to see the presentation because the superintendent asked the children to perform during a staff development day. Belinda and the other students received recognition. It gave them exposure and respect. The teachers who saw them perform had high expectations and supported them. Teachers knew who they were and treated them very well. Belinda remembers these feelings were different from her early school years.

> After that, I remember in every class the teachers all said something when they saw me in their class. They recognized me in front of the class. They explained to the whole class who I was and what I did. They said they were very proud to have me in their class. That made me feel real good and very important. (BM, 255–260)

Belinda enjoyed high school and made the most of it. Mr. G. offered a simple explanation:

> By the time she got to ninth grade she refused to take no for an answer. When she got to high school she already knew that she had rights, and she demanded equal treatment. She knew that she could be an honor student. She didn't want to be treated special, but she wanted to be treated just the same as everybody else. She sort of reached a mini-level of self-actualization. She came to realize who she

75

was and how important she was. And I think she became a fighter for the underdog. She was trying to prove that we were all the same. (RG: 96–107)

Belinda's parents did not understand what the presentations really meant. To this day, Belinda said, "My parents think that the migrant presentations were the main reason why I got accepted to the CAMP program. They didn't understand the concept" (BM, 342–345).

High school was also different because the last year she migrated was her freshman year. After that she never left early, and she participated in many extra curricular activities. She competed in literary events such as poetry, spelling, and other events. From then on she worked at McDougal's during the summer. She was glad she did not have to go work in the fields anymore. "It didn't compare to working in the fields. I would still give my mom most of what I earned to help them out" (BM, 350–353). Though we knew what the answer would be, we asked which job she liked more, McDougal's or the fields. Belinda said tentatively,

Honestly? I would rather work at McDougal's. Working in the fields was hard work, but that wasn't the worst of it. I worried about leaving school early, and not knowing where we were going to live. The housing was always terrible no matter where we went. It was an adventure. We knew we were going to work, but we didn't know if it was going to be a good year. When I was in high school my parents stopped going north because it wasn't worth going anymore. *Ya no teníamos manos* [we didn't have any working hands] because all my older brothers and sisters were gone except Erica and me. (BM, 401–412)

Everything Belinda had hoped for in elementary and junior high finally became a reality in high school. She did not dread the first day of school anymore or worry about her schedule. She was popular and respected. She was in advanced and honors classes. Her teachers supported her and inspired her. Her French teacher was very nice to her, and Belinda talked about her fondly. "I always did so well in her class. She would always give me credit and recognition. She was always very nice to me" (BM, 413–415). She also had another teacher who encouraged her to be a teacher. "She always wanted me to be a teacher. She would tell me I needed to be a teacher because she knew I had it in me. I was in her best class" (BM: 419–421).

Overall, she said she was treated fairly in high school. The only thing she resented was not being allowed to get into the GT English class. That class was still reserved for students who had certain achievement test scores. Belinda knew those requirements, but she still tried to get in. She shared the following anecdote:

One of the things I felt bad about in high school was that I wanted to be in GT English with Ms. Davila. I had Ms. Andrews for advanced English, but I wanted to be in that GT class. The counselor did not let me change because he said I didn't have good achievement test scores. I knew I could do just as well as all the students that were in that class. I had a 100 average in all my four advanced English classes that I took in high school. I kept telling him that I could do GT work and I would show him if he just gave me a chance. He refused to change me because of my scores. (BM: 427–437)

Belinda could not wait to graduate. It was almost like she wanted to skip all the formalities and go on to college. She did not want all the traditional celebrations. Belinda did not want her parents to spend any money like they did for the other children. "I remember my mom would go buy *cabrito* [kid goat], bake a cake, and invite all the family and friends for a big celebration. I didn't want a big *fiesta,* but she still had a small dinner for me" (BM, 437–439). Belinda was excited about her graduation, and she reminded one of the authors that he was there that evening. She said, "Graduation was a good feeling, it was a feeling of accomplishment" (BM: 437–439).

She was an honor graduate with a 95.2 average. She was awarded several scholarships, and she was accepted to all the colleges to which she applied. Belinda was accepted to George Washington University in Washington, D.C., and received a scholarship to the medical school program. "I was going to study under the guidance of a professor doctor for seven years and go into residency afterward" (BM, 463–473).

She was never really sure if she wanted to go into medicine. She was invited to visit the campus when she was a senior and had a bad experience on the trip. There was a blizzard, and she got stranded at the airport. "I got lost and scared. My mom cried a lot and she didn't want me to go so far away. I wonder what that could have been like. I'm happy now anyway" (BM, 387–392).

Belinda was also offered a scholarship to another university. Though it was her second choice, she chose St. Edwards University in Austin, TX, when she was accepted to the CAMP program.

> I remember when I first got to St. Ed's. We were known as the CAMPers. We always hung around together. We all got real close during the three weeks we spent together for orientation. That was part of the program before we started classes. We had a closing ceremony, and every year they picked a student to deliver the closing speech. That year they chose me. I gave my migrant speech and got a lot of compliments. The professors liked it and asked me to give another speech for the student leadership program. (BM, 463–473)

Belinda graduated from college in May 1997 with a greater than 3.0 grade point average. She earned a bachelor of science degree with a major in Spanish and international business. She lived on campus because it was required for CAMP students the first year. She moved to an apartment with some friends as soon as she could. Though she received financial help, she started working the second semester of her freshman year because she wanted to help her parents. She worked all through school and carried a full load of classes all the time. She worked as a cashier at a retail store, a telephone operator, and a bank teller. Belinda never doubted she would finish and earn her degree, but it was not easy.

When she finished she did not want to go to the graduation because her parents were not going to be there. Her mother had just gone through surgery and her father had a new job. She knew he did not want to ask for time off and jeopardize his job. Belinda decided not to go to make it easier on them. They were going to feel bad because they could not come, and she knew she would be sad also. When the graduation date got close, her boyfriend convinced her to go.

> He told me I had worked so hard to earn this degree and that I needed to give it closure. He told me I should go because I would regret it later. So I decided to go, and it was so ugly and sad. At the end everybody turned back and looked up to the upper level to find their parents, family, and friends. I had no one to look for except my

boyfriend, and I couldn't find him. I felt so sad especially when we walked out and everybody was hugging their parents. (BM, 502–513)

She and her boyfriend drove home from Austin after graduation. Her parents were very happy when she got home that night. Everything was ready for the *fiesta*. Her mother bought her a graduation gift.

Mom had bought me a little *medalla con la Virgen de Guadalupe* [medallion of the Virgin of Guadalupe] for graduation. I could see and feel their pride. They were so proud of me. I am the first one to earn a bachelor's degree in my family. (BM, 515–516)

Belinda had the ability to bear and draw strength from her life disappointments. As she grew older, her family was often in a position of not being able to "be there" for her. Belinda persevered through these disappointments and was able to succeed—where her primary support system as a youth was initially her family, as a young adult, she was able to gain strength from her reputation, achievements, and her resolute inner self.

Benito's School Life and Experiences

Benito is a product of the Rio Grande City Independent School District. He attended Norris Elementary (Head Start through grade 4), Redfield Intermediate (grades 5 and 6), and Redfield Jr. High (grades 7 and 8). He graduated from Redfield High School in 1979. Today, Rio Grande City CISD is a small Class 5A school district with about 8,000 students. It has grown since Benito graduated 18 years ago.

Benito has few but meaningful memories of his early childhood school years. He was frightened when he started kindergarten because he did not speak English. "English has always been my second language and I struggled. I didn't like it because we had to take naps and I didn't want to sleep" (BG: 120–124)

In elementary, there were not many sections, so students were either in the high, medium, or low group. Benito was always with the "better group" in elementary. The only teacher he mentioned was his fourth-grade teacher, but only because that was the year when all his friends came together. "A group of us basically stayed together since fourth grade. It was always Roland, Santiago, Billy, Elmo, Gerardo, and myself"

(BG, 129–143). They are still very close friends and get together every year.

When they went to fifth grade, Redfield Intermediate was much bigger, and they split up. It was more competitive, and Benito and some of his friends were no longer in the more "advanced groups." In junior high it was more of the same. He was never placed in the top section. He says that somehow he was always in the third section.

> There were sections 7–1a, 7–1b, 7–2a, and so on. I was always in the 2a section. Of course I always felt that obviously it was because of who I was, all the 7–1as and 7–1bs were all the kids whose parents were a little bit better and that sort of thing. (BG, 177–185)

In the eighth grade, he wanted to take Algebra, but he was not allowed to take it by his math teacher.

> Mr. Pérez said I was just an average student and I was not allowed to register because I didn't have the scores. I never had a chance because it was only going to be one class, and I was three classes down. I remember that it was the superintendent's son, and of course the principal's son, and other people like that [in Algebra]. (BG, 187–193)

Needless to say, Benito was disappointed. He knew he had better scores than some students that got in. As a freshman he tried to take Algebra, but Mr. Pérez again discouraged him. Benito started to doubt himself. "I began to think that maybe he was right and that I was just an average student" BG, 201–203. Instead, he took Introduction to Algebra with an excellent teacher. He struggled his freshman year but learned his concepts well. Consequently, he breezed through Algebra I and II, and Geometry. "The funny thing is that one of my 'rich' friends took algebra in the eighth grade and didn't pass, his freshman year and didn't pass, and his sophomore year and didn't pass it" (BG, 218–225).

Benito did well in high school. Though his counselor tried to guide him into the vocational program because he was not "college material," he took the college prep courses and graduated with an 86.55 average.

> I remember going to the counselor and telling her I wanted to go to college and she told me that I should consider a vocational school and

that sort of thing. Of course at that time I didn't know any better, I just wanted to go play football and I wasn't thinking of any school per se. (BG, 267–281)

If there was anything he felt totally confident about, it was his ability to play football. He was an outstanding football player and earned All Valley honors his junior and senior years. As a senior he was selected to the All State team. Benito was offered a football scholarship and went on to play football at Sul Ross State University in Alpine, Texas. After four years Benito graduated and earned his BA degree in Liberal Arts in 1983.

Benito became interested in law school his junior year in college. On one of his trips back home, he ran into a good friend from high school. Benito said "*René me dio cuerda de law school* [René cranked me up about law school]" (BG, 304–304). He began to think about it seriously when another friend, Roel Blanco, told him about the Council on Legal Education Opportunities (CLEO) program and encouraged him to pursue it.

Upon graduation he picked up an application from a college counselor and made arrangements to take the Law School Admission Test (LSAT). He didn't prepare for the test. He simply reviewed the sample questions on the application booklet. According to him,

I didn't know any better so that was the only booklet that I studied. I didn't know at that time that there were review courses you could pay money and go for a week or two. I went and took the test based on that little booklet. (BG, 310–314)

He took the test in Odessa, Texas. There were over 200 people taking the test and Benito is sure they were all White except him. He scored a 20 on a scale of 1–50. The mean score for Hispanics that year was 22. He applied to four law schools (Texas Tech, University of Houston, The University of Texas at Austin, and St. Mary's) and was rejected by all of them.

Benito was disappointed and discouraged. He forgot about law school and considered teaching and coaching. He was offered a teaching position at the high school in his hometown, but opted to go back to Sul Ross to work on a master's in counseling. Then he got a call from the executive director of the CLEO program. He had received a letter inviting him to participate in the CLEO program, but threw it away when he was not accepted to any school. Benito thought it was fate.

> I had gone home to see Mom. I was supposed to take one of my cousins to McAllen, but she changed her mind. I went back home and I heard my Mom struggling on the phone with someone. I walked in just in time because it was the executive director of the CLEO program. She wanted to know why I had not responded to the letter, and I explained why. (BG, 387–398)

Benito had assumed that the invitation to participate in the CLEO program was contingent upon his acceptance to law school. To the contrary, Ms. Rosas explained that the program was designed for applicants like him. It was for those who had not been accepted, but showed potential. Ms. Rosas told Benito that he had been awarded a fellowship. The invitation was still open, but he had to be in Topeka, Kansas, two days later. Benito was elated and quickly said, "I'll take it! That was the chance I needed" (BG, 148–154). Within minutes, he made a decision that changed the course of his life. "I packed the only pair of pants I had brought with me and drove off to Del Rio, Texas, to say goodbye to my girlfriend [future wife] and moved out of the 'fish bowl' [apartment] in Alpine" (BG, 148–154).

Benito was in Topeka two days later on June 6, 1983. There were about 35 participants at the institute. They were all Hispanic and African American. Benito remembered the welcome.

> You are here because we think you have what it takes to be a lawyer. Some of you are here because you have good GPAs but bad LSAT scores, and some of you have very good LSAT scores but low GPAs. Most of you have not been accepted to any law school. If you get through our program we guarantee you placement in one of the top three schools of your choice, and we'll give you a $1,000.00 scholarship each year. (BG, 402–417)

Benito got through the program and chose to go to the Thurgood Marshall School of Law in Houston, Texas.

Benito experienced many hardships in school as a result of discrimination. However, it was notable that the role played by low teacher expectations in blocking the development of students was also key in motivating the attention of the migrant student when it was high and expressed.

Sonia's School Life and Experiences

The school experiences that Sonia had in her home-base school did not happen in isolation to those she had in the state of Washington. For the purpose of this study, we chose to discuss them separately, though they occurred simultaneously from year to year. Both are vital to this study and must be given equal attention.

Sonia led two lives in two different places. Half the year she lived in the comfort of her home in Alamo, Texas, and went to school with her friends in her home-base school. The other half she lived in migrant labor camps, picking asparagus, berries, and cucumbers, and attending school in Washington wherever she could.

On the surface, Sonia's experiences at school appeared very similar to those of any other student. She was excited but frightened about going to school. She cried like many other 4-year-olds when her parents dropped her off at school her first day.

> I remember one year, but I'm not sure if it was kinder or pre-kinder, that I went. My mom dropped me off, and I was kind of scared and I started crying, 'cause I was all . . . I didn't want to be alone with people I didn't know. So I started crying, and she left 'cause the next thing I knew she wasn't there. I was just still crying, but then this little girl next to me told me that nothing was going to happen. (SR, 290–297).

Sonia's home-base school was in Pharr, San Juan, Alamo (PSJA), but she also attended several schools in the state of Washington. Every year she withdrew from school early (except her seventh-grade and senior years) to make the family's annual trip to *los trabajos* (the jobs) late in March.

The first time we interviewed Sonia was at Sunset labor camp in Washington. Seated at the small kitchen table she had just cleaned, we asked Sonia, "How does it feel to leave school early every year? You have done it since you were in pre-kinder." She replied,

> Oh . . . it's, well, it's hard because . . . actually, sometimes I feel angry 'cause I have to leave all my friends, everything . . . it's towards the

end of the year, you start making plans . . . the best things happen at the end of the year, the dances, the parties. I have never been here for a prom. (SR, 154–158)

That was how the school year came to an end for Sonia every year. Though she might have felt anger initially, she was neither bitter nor resentful. She never discussed her feelings with her parents or any of her siblings. She did not hold it against her parents at all. "Well, it's not their fault. It's just the way things are. Well, 'cause it's not something that they chose for us" (SR, 165–167). She accepts it because that is the only way she knows how to cope with it.

Well, I forget about it. It's just like . . . that's life. I got used to it. You know? You're going to have fun over here also. You have to get used to the people first, and then you start enjoying it and stuff. (SR, 176–179)

What kept her going was that she knew it was just a matter of time before she stopped making the trip with her parents. Her "ticket out" was graduation from high school and enrollment in college.

A review of her experiences in school elucidated her remarkable adventure through an educational system not designed to meet the needs of highly mobile students like Sonia.

For Sonia, mobility was not restricted to her annual trips to Washington State as a migrant farm worker. During her early school years (prekindergarten through fourth grade), she attended three different elementary schools while her parents built their home. Like many migrant families, they built their home themselves. Most did it on a piecemeal basis—usually from year to year if they had money left over from their trip north. Sonia started at Ferris Elementary, then moved to Franco, to Bowers, and then finally back to Ferris for fourth and fifth grades. She went to Elmo Middle School for grades 6, 7, and 8. She was never in one place long enough to establish meaningful relationships with her peers. Perhaps that is why she does not have memories of specific friends.

In first grade I left all my friends, you know, I didn't want to go to this other school 'cause all my friends were at this school. And then in fourth grade, they moved me back to Ferris. That was a different school. And then I left all my friends that were from Bowers. I left them behind and I didn't want to go to Ferris, because I didn't know anybody there. (SR, 368–374)

Nostalgically, she reminisced about several incidents and memories still clear in her mind. She remembered second grade, but she did not remember the teacher. She had to leave her regular classroom for part of the day.

When I was in second grade, I moved . . . 'cause my father was building our house. We moved farther out of town, so I had to go to a different elementary. I had this teacher I don't remember, but I remember that I would leave during her class. I think it was during the reading in English. I would go to a different class, but I never knew why. They were third graders, or fourth graders or something like that. I would go next door and they were all older than me, but I don't remember why. I just never knew why. (SR, 403–411)

She could not explain why, but our guess is that she was either reading significantly above grade level or she was in a multi-age remedial reading pullout program commonly provided for migrant students during that time. She had very fond memories of her fourth grade year.

I think it was in fourth grade when we moved into the house . . . we moved back to the house, and then I had to just walk to school again. 'Cause I went back to Ferris, my friends from fourth grade, they're the ones that I have right now. . . .Our teacher's name was Ms. Stasney. She was really nice....We got to know each other . . . and we would . . . she would do a lot of fun stuff. We had a Christmas party and stuff. She got us involved, like in . . . we had a say in what we could do with the room and stuff. We got to decorate it and stuff. She would let, like, ask for our help. We were involved in the decisions. (SR, 421–431)

Sonia remembers fifth grade because she got there late

and they put me in the low class. I was in there with a bunch of *burros* [dummies]. They didn't try at all. They wouldn't try. . . .They wouldn't bother trying 'cause they knew the teacher would tell them how to do it. I didn't stay in this class very long. They moved me to Ms. Elsa's class where I was supposed to be anyway. (SR, 443–451)

According to Sonia, fifth grade turned out to be her best year in elementary. "I think it's 'cause I wasn't moving any more. I was already there, and I had my friends from fourth grade. We had different teachers, but we would still meet outside, and we would still have lunch together and stuff" (SR, 459–462).

Sonia came back to school late in the fall every year. Many times migrant students ended up in newly formed classrooms if the others were full. Sonia said that somehow she was always with the "best teacher" in elementary.

Everyone knew who the best teacher was, and well . . . if you were not in that classroom you weren't very smart. I don't know if it was the teacher or the group. It was the teacher who had the more advanced students . . . I know I was not GT, but I was with that group. (SR, 472–476)

When she moved to middle school it was different. She had to manipulate the system to make sure she stayed with the more challenging group. The only way to stay with her group was to join the band. "It was an all-band student class, so I joined the band. I played drums, that was the only instrument left. I decided I wanted to stay in this class . . . to be in a class that was more challenging" (SR, 484–487). Sonia was resourceful and ingenious when she had to be. She submitted herself to things she really did not want to do (join the band and play drums) as a means to an end.

When they arrived in Washington, they were immediately enrolled in school to finish the school year. They also went to school in Washington in the fall before they came back to Texas. In some places like Mabton, Connell, Pasco, and Meridian, Washington, programs were in place to assist migrant students. Sonia's sister, Ana, felt more comfortable in Washington schools than in her home school in Texas. "Though we were in separate classrooms many times, the teachers really cared and took care of us. In Texas, there were too many of us [migrant students], and we were just numbers. (AR, 187–190)

Sonia remembered that they were all placed in segregated classrooms.

The schools were not prepared for the sudden influx of migrant students coming into their districts though they had been coming to Washington for generations. Highly impacted schools depended on migrant programs to take care of these students. Sonia seemed to remember her experiences in Washington much better.

> We went to Mabton, and from there I do remember my first-grade teacher, my second-grade teacher, my third-grade teacher. I remember them 'cause all the migrants were in one class together. We made friends right there. And we all stuck together (first, second, third). And then fifth grade is when they decided to separate us and get us with the regular students. But we had made a lot of friends. We were all from Texas . . . most of us from the Valley. (SR, 554–562)

Sonia felt secure with her friends. They had grown used to being with each other. They were all in a new and strange place together, far from home, and with teachers and students they did not know.

> We knew each other. We were comfortable with each other. We did not interact with the regular students very much because we didn't do things together. We had lunch together, but we would sit, like, with the teachers. Each teacher and her class sat at a table. So, we would sit together, all of us. And then they would look at us because we would be talking in Spanish. And they would look at us kind of weird also. But, we didn't mind. They didn't understand us, but we understood whatever they said. So we felt like we had an advantage. We can speak two languages. We have two different cultures and stuff. We've got the best of two worlds. (SR, 567–587)

Sonia did not feel inferior or less capable than the "regular students." When other students questioned her ability, she was determined to show them that she was just as capable or better than they. These challenges motivated her. "When they made fun of us I guess we all always wanted to show them that . . . Yeah, we can do it. And we are smarter. We didn't feel uncomfortable so we continued to keep good grades and stuff" (SR, 576–580).

Migrant students were not immune to the problems that came with adolescence. These problems were compounded by the demands they experienced in middle and high school. However, migrant students like Sonia, who were highly mobile, had to surmount odds many other students did not. Many migrant students could survive relatively well in elementary school. Their chances of success in secondary were progressively less likely due to the demands of their lifestyle coupled with the school system's ineptitude to meet their unique needs.

The problem was twofold. On the one hand, as migrant children got older, they were expected to work first and go to school second. Work was the primary reason they made the trip north. On the other hand, most high schools continued to be extremely traditional in the way they were organized and structured. High schools required certain number of Carnegie units in order to earn a diploma. Obviously, if students were not in school, they did not earn credit. A migrant student's lifestyle was far from traditional. Sonia's high school in Texas was sensitive to the needs of migrant students. Her principal, Mr. Rodríguez, was very much aware of their special needs.

> We have about 700 migrant students. Our school district has one of the largest migrant student populations in the state, if not the largest. We make special arrangements for migrant students to make up credits before they leave in the spring or when they come back in the fall. We also work closely with other states to make sure they get credit for classes they take over there. (Mr R, 23–30)

Migrant students at Valley High School were lucky they had a principal who was sensitive. One of the authors worked with migrant students who were credit deficient in other states. As he coordinated course work for students from Texas high schools, he dealt with several principals and counselors who were reluctant to accept credits from anywhere else. Though the educational system was not designed for the non-traditional student, educators like Sonia's principal could make a difference individually.

Nonetheless, while migrant students were trying to settle into their new classes they were also trying to learn material and concepts they had missed. "It seems like we are always trying to catch up" (SR, 570–571). Those who refused to stay behind found ways to earn credits any way they could. There were several programs available to help them stay abreast. They could earn credits by going to summer school or night school in receiving states. Interstate coordination was vital because one of the main reasons migrant students lost credits was poor record keeping. Many students also earned credit through correspondence courses, enrolling in distance learning courses via satellite, or independent courses through the Portable Assisted Sequence Studies (PASS) program.

Whatever program they chose, they had to continue to work in the fields with their parents. In Sonia's case, she went to night school when she was older because she and her brothers and sister had to help their parents during the day. According to her sister,

> Even when we were going to elementary school, we had to wake up real early, work an hour or two, come back to the camp, take a shower, and run to catch the bus with the rest of the kids. (AR, 580–584)

By the time migrant children like Sonia arrived at school, they had been up and working for a few hours.

Except for her seventh-grade and senior years, Sonia left early and come back late every school year. We asked Sonia, "What would you rather do? Leave early or come back late?" If it was up to her she would rather not go at all.

> I don't want to go. It's a lot of hard work. I would rather leave early and come back to Texas the first day. You don't have to make up work. You just start with everybody. And well, you get your classes, the ones that you want. And it's like . . . well, right now, I still need one fourth of Spanish II because when we were over there, since they're not in block scheduling, I missed out . . . and I'm taking that so I can graduate in the advanced program. (SR, 598–606)

Sonia had not only kept up, but she managed to stay ahead. At the end of her junior year she had every credit she needed to be a senior and was on track to graduate with an advanced program diploma. Keeping up with her schoolwork was not the only reason she opted to take course work through the PASS program. She completed three courses: World History, Health, and Algebra II. She wanted to do well in school but she said she took the PASS courses "to help my parents out picking asparagus. We would go to work for 4 hours (from 7:00 to 11:00). Then we would go to school after lunch. We took classes through PASS in night school" (SR, 635–640).

However, when the asparagus was at peak season, there were days they did not go to night school. Ana remembered,

> sometimes my father would keep us because there was so much aspar-agus to cut. And it's funny, but I remember wanting to go to school. We would cry if my Dad would not let us go. That was like our only social time. (AR, 236–240)

Sonia's senior year was different. For seventeen years, she made the annual trip to Washington to pick asparagus, strawberries, raspberries and cucumbers. This was the first time in her life that she did not travel to Washington with her parents. She had never experienced a summer in her home in Alamo, Texas. All her brothers and her sister graduated from high schools in Washington. She was the first in her family to graduate from Valley High School, and unfortunately, also the first not to have her parents present at the ceremony because they were picking asparagus in Washington. We asked Mr. and Mrs. Ramírez if they were coming back for Sonia's graduation. As much as they wanted to come, they said they could not afford it. "*Si venimos por unos días, perdemos el trabajo* [If we come for a few days, we will lose our jobs]" (FR, 93–95). Sonia gradu-ated from Valley High School on May 31, 1997. She was in the advanced program and graduated in the top third of her class (202 of 637) with an 82 overall average.

Valley High School is one of two high schools in the PSJA Indepen-dent School District. This school district serves three communities locat-ed in the Rio Grande Valley in deep south Texas, about 8 miles north of the Texas and México border. Valley High School is surrounded by homes on three sides and ironically by vast fields of vegetables on the south side. Even when migrant students sit in class, they can look out the window and possibly see family and friends working in the fields. It is a large campus with well over 30 buildings and about 2,800 students in grades 9–12. The faculty consists of about 165 professionals and 70 paraprofessionals (TEA, 1997). In terms of the school's demographics, Hispanic students make up 98% percent of the student population and Anglo students make up the other 2%. Of the Hispanic students, 25%

have been identified as migrant, 29% as limited English proficient (LEP), and 77% as economically disadvantaged (TEA, 1997).

We went to Sonia's graduation ceremony. We drove from Austin that morning and stopped by her house before she left for the stadium. We wanted to make sure we spoke with her before the ceremony because we were afraid we would not be able to find her in the crowd of over 600 graduates. We stopped at a local store and carefully picked a graduation card and a bright yellow rose for her. Sonia was expecting us. Ana, her sister, answered the door and invited us in. Sonia was getting ready, but came out to the living room to greet us. We did not stay very long. We told her we would try to find her after the ceremony, but it was going to be hard.

We knew her parents were not coming, but we thought they might surprise Sonia—deep down inside we were hoping they would come to see their youngest daughter graduate. They were 2,300 miles away at the time Sonia walked across the stage to receive her diploma, probably on their way back to the camp from a long day of picking asparagus.

VI
THE MENTORS—ENVIRONMENTAL RESOURCES

⊸

The Human Connection: "You can! I will help you"

It has been said that human beings have two hands—to help each other. The migrant students were able to find those helping hands—the support and resources they needed to achieve their potential and to grow, in spite of life's challenges and the adverse economic circumstances of their childhood.

Belinda's Mentors: "If it hadn't been for you"

In junior high, Belinda's major concern was still her schedule. She wondered what kind of classes she was going to get. She wanted more than just the regular classes. She wanted to be in the advanced and honors classes, but not because she wanted the harder work or the challenge. She simply wanted to prove she could do just as well as the other students. She wondered if "it was because I didn't have the money or I didn't wear the nice clothes? It wasn't fair. If you had money you were with one group, and if you didn't, you were with the other" (BM, 162–164). Belinda's tone changed as she told one of the authors, "That's the year when you came in the picture, into my life. I remember telling Mr. G. I wanted to be in his science class, and he told me to go talk to you, the counselor" (BM, 175–177).

Mr. G. told her to talk to one of the authors, the counselor, because he knew she would be placed in his class. This was a science class for GT students. Belinda was not the only student who was not officially labeled GT assigned to that class. The teacher said these were students "who were misunderstood, or who were down on their luck, or migrants, or LEP children. Many of these students wound up in my classes" (RG, 45–48).

All the kids affectionately called this particular teacher Mr. G., short for García. He taught science and theater arts. He was very popular and well liked by the students. Students felt good in his classes. He was very proud of Belinda and had fond memories of her.

> I'll never forget Belinda. She was a go-getter, she was determined, she was a dreamer, and an achiever. Those are things I always noticed in her. From day one, she had that gleam in her eyes. But one thing that stands out that I'll never forget about her is that when she was a seventh grader, she was tall, she was gauntly, and she was very thin. She stuck out like that ugly duckling, but there was something about her that told me something good was going to happen. (RG, 23–34)

Belinda said the migrant conference presentations influenced her future indirectly. She believes that was the main reason why her parents did not insist that she stay close to home and go to a vocational school. She said,

> I remember you (one of the authors) went to my house to talk to my parents. They couldn't believe what you were telling them about me. You told them I could be a doctor, "*ella puede ser abogada, puede ser lo que quiera* [she can be a lawyer, she can be whatever she wants]." My dad was amazed and asked, "*¿usted cree* [you think so]?" It was then when they accepted that I was going to college and it didn't matter where. Mr. García and you were the main difference in my life. If it hadn't been for you two, I would just be a secretary. I would have gone to vocational school. (BM, 3–15)

When she felt pressure and doubt, she had someone to talk to. In college Belinda had a professor who helped her out. He helped her stay focused.

I would always go to Dr. García when I was down or worried about something. He would encourage me. He would say *"usted puede señorita Belinda, usted no se achicopale, usted para delante* [you can do it Belinda, don't you get down on yourself, you go forward]." He kept me going when things were rough. (BM, 486–497)

Benito's Mentor: "He turned my life around"

Benito did not have any memories of teachers who inspired or motivated him, but responded to these negative experiences in a positive way. He responded in his own *terco* (stubborn) way and proved them wrong. When his algebra teacher told him he was not smart enough to take his class, that inspired Benito. When the high school counselor tried to put him in the vocational track because he was not "college material," he chose the college prep courses just to show her otherwise.

He remembered a teacher who had a reputation for spanking students with *un palo de escoba* (a broomstick). Benito saw him spank a classmate. "This teacher was a lefty, and he spanked this student hard with the broomstick. Everything we had heard about him was true, but he was a good science teacher" (BG, 235–240)

However, Benito identified three people who had a significant impact on his life. Number one on his list was obviously his mother. Besides his mother, two other individuals made a big difference in his life: a high school football coach and a college professor.

Benito's motivation in school came from athletics, his teammates, and his coaches. Several coaches made a difference in Benito's life when he was in high school. However, the one that had the most impact on Benito was Coach Ponce. When Oscar Ponce came to Rio Grande City as the head football coach, Benito was a sophomore. Initially, he and Benito did not get along well, but their relationship changed as time passed. Coach Ponce took care of Benito, and helped him in many ways. Benito acknowledged that he was the key person in his life, other than his mother.

Coach Ponce was the main difference for me. When he first came in we had a bad clash, so much so that I almost quit athletics as a result. However, by the time I finished high school he was like a father to me, and he helped me through some personal problems. He was the one person without question of all the coaches that was the main difference for me. He showed me discipline. I think encouragement has come along the way from several sources. But you know, when Coach Ponce did some of the things for me, I don't know why he did it. I don't think he did it because he was a coach. I think he did it more because he was a Christian. He did some things that most teachers don't do. Spending his own money, gas, his car, and his time to take me to college. Giving me advice like a father I never had. He turned my life around. I think the reason Oscar sort of gave me special attention was because he didn't have his dad either. He was raised by his mom. He had been raised very poor also. He used to tell me that he saw many similarities between us. I don't know whether he felt sorry for me, but he knew that I needed the help. He was there at that critical time when I was a teenager getting ready to graduate from high school. That was real important and I think he's one of the key people that actually touched that nerve to open my eyes a little bit more. (BG, 37–43)

Benito still keeps in touch with his coach. He named his second son Oscar after the person that made the greatest difference in his life. Benito earned a B.A. degree from Sul Ross State University in 1983. The university did not offer any scholarships, but they helped him with housing. He lived on campus, but not in a dormitory. Instead, he was allowed to stay at the athletic field house. He decided to quit playing after sustaining a knee injury early his sophomore year. That spring he moved to a small apartment he shared with Gerardo, a childhood friend. Living off campus was not much better than the field house. They lived in a small one-bedroom apartment with barely enough room for their beds. They did not have a kitchen. They affectionately called their apartment the "fish bowl." For almost three years they cooked on an electric hot plate and washed dishes in the restroom sink. They each paid $50 rent per month.

In college, Dr. Bernal took Coach Ponce's place as Benito's mentor and advisor. He encouraged and inspired Benito the same way Coach Ponce had. He helped him believe in himself, and he urged him to go to law school.

Benito's initial interest was in biology, but he graduated with a major in English and Spanish. In college he took several classes with Dr. Bernal, the only Hispanic professor at Sul Ross State University at the time. Dr. Bernal became Benito's mentor and his guardian angel. He inspired him and guided him much the same way Coach Ponce did when he was in high school. Coincidentally, Dr. Bernal's and Benito's backgrounds were also very similar. He helped Benito get a couple of scholarships from the Spanish department. He was Benito's advocate. Benito remembered,

> There was this particular scholarship. It was the scholarship for the Liberal Arts department. Every department head would submit the names, and this was like the biggest scholarship as far as honor and prestige. Dr. Bernal submitted my name from his department and the dean of the Liberal Arts department submitted Lana's. She was from Copperas Cove. It came down to her and me. Of course, she got it. There was no question that she deserved it more than I did in the sense that she had better grades. I remember this because Dr. Bernal afterwards was very intense. If you know him, he is pretty blunt about the way he sees and says things. He was really upset about it because he felt that I should be the one to get it, though this girl had better grades than I did. He felt this girl could afford college. She had her parents who were supporting her through college and I didn't. Dr. Bernal's biggest argument was that I needed it more. (BG, 93–110)

Benito's grades were better than average. His grade point average was 3.30 when he graduated. He was very active as the president of the Spanish club. Dr. Bernal was the sponsor of the club. He said Benito "was the best president that the Spanish Club has ever had. In fact, we had so much money in the treasury that the group took a trip to México City" (AB, 112–114).

Dr. Bernal thinks highly of Benito. He said, "Benito García is one person I admire greatly in this world. He is one of my success stories. I feel proud of students such as him who have gone on to carve a name for themselves in society" (AB, 115–117).

Sonia's Mentors:
"They were always encouraging us to do our best"

Sonia remembers several teachers in middle school, but Ms. Barnes had the greatest impact on her. "In eighth grade our math teacher was Ms.

Barnes. She made everything really fun. She made everything a song and stuff . . . she always had a story. And she had tunes so you could remember the negatives and positives" (SR: 489–492).

Though she said she liked all her teachers in high school, a couple of teachers were more inspiring to her. "I really liked Mr. Avalos, who had taught me Geometry and he was my Algebra teacher there. He was really nice also" (SR, 508–510). Sonia said she could not take pre-calculus with him because of a conflict in her schedule. Mr. Avalos knew Sonia would do well because she had "exceptional ability, drive, and is very persistent. She never gives up" (Mr. A, 56). After we spoke to Mr. Avalos, we talked to Mr. Reyes, her pre-calculus teacher. It was almost as if he had met with Mr. Avalos and they had agreed to say the same things about Sonia. "She is very well behaved, has great desire, and an excellent work ethic" (Mr. A, 59).

Sonia is a persistent individual who is determined to follow in her older sister's footsteps. She did not hesitate to admit that her sister, Ana, was her role model.

Well, she's my sister and she has gone through college. She's done it on her own. She's been able to go through school and complete it and stuff. So she's successful right now. What she's wanted to do, she's accomplished it. I want to follow in her footsteps. Maybe even try to beat her. She encourages me to study . . . she's the one who told me to look for a college outside of the Valley. That it's a different experience, which it really helps to move away from home. I admire my sister, but I want to do better than her and surpass her accomplishments. (SR, 235–246)

Though Ana is Sonia's role model, she was also her contender. Her mother said,

Sonia todo el tiempo fue muy celosa. Cuando hablábamos de Ana, ella decía, "Pues yo quiero estudiar para ser más que ella" [Sonia was always jealous. When we talked about Ana, she would say, "I want to study so I can be better than her"]. (AR, 22–25)

Ana set the standards and expectations. Her father used her as the measuring stick to motivate the other children, especially Sonia. Sonia lived under the shadow of her older sister. Mr. Ramírez constantly compared them until Ana intervened. "I always knew that was unhealthy. And I remember I told my dad, 'Don't do that 'cause . . . you know, she's her own person, and I'm . . . my own person'" (AR, 110–113). Ana knows Sonia will do as well and better than her, and she wants to help her do it. "I've always told her that, you know, if she needs anything, she could come to me" (AR, 118–120).

We never heard Sonia complain or make excuses about school or work. She knows she will break away from the migrant cycle she has been locked into since birth. Though she is proud of it, it is an oppressive lifestyle she looks forward to changing. When we asked her why she was so sure she would succeed, she simply said,

> Some students succeed in school, in spite of the odds against them. I get out of school early to go work, and come back late in the fall. I go to schools in another state. I think I am doing well because . . . well, I know that it's important for me to get my education. If . . . unless I want to continue like my parents, who keep coming down here.

There is mutual respect between Sonia and her sister Ana. Ana admires Sonia as much as Sonia admires her. Ana said,

> Sonia always had a good sense of direction, academically and socially. Sonia is very sensitive. She gets along with other people. She likes to have a good time. She, at times, is very quiet and reserved, but she gets her work done . . . she's very dependable and hard-working. She has this arthritis problem and there are a lot of things that she can't do physically because of that. I know she's very outgoing. More so than maybe I was at her age. Even though she might think she's not. (AR, 82–92)

The place occupied by the mentors in the lives of the migrant students necessarily complemented that held by their supportive extended families. Without either component, the successful outcomes for the students would not have been realized—at least in the ways they were realized with the inputs from both support groups.

VII
THE PRESENT—SUCCESS AGAINST ALL ODDS

～

NO ONE WOULD HAVE IMAGINED THAT, AGAINST ALL ODDS, THESE MIGRANT students would be who they are today. The three have become bright stars in the dark sky of anonymous, ceaselessly toiling migrant workers. They are resilient, durable, playful, free and committed to help others to attempt the impossible—to achieve a better life in spite of life's challenges and the adverse economic circumstances of their childhood.

Belinda

> "The turning point in my life: when I started to feel proud of myself, my parents, my family, and our lifestyle."

Belinda's participation in the migrant conference presentations gave her a feeling of accomplishment and confidence. It also gave her a sense of power and inner strength to overcome any obstacles and barriers. Most importantly, Belinda said,

> Those presentations at the migrant conferences brought closure to my migrant life. That is not to say that I was going to put it behind and out of my mind. On the contrary, I'll never forget it . . . there's no way. It is part of me and that's who I am. (BM, 290–293)

Belinda is now very proud of the way she grew up. She felt ashamed of being a migrant all through school. She was embarrassed that her parents did not speak English. "I remember many times I didn't want to go with my mom to the store because I had to be the interpreter all the time" (BM: 216–220).

These negative feelings began to change when she got to high school. "I started to feel proud of myself, my parents, my family, and our lifestyle. When I was getting ready to go off to college I realized what my parents meant to me, and how much they cared about me" (BM, 731–742).

Belinda's View of Success and Reflection

Belinda's definition of success:

> To me success was or is, using your words [the author and counselor], just being able to break the cycle. The cycle of migrancy, just breaking away from that nomadic lifestyle. Being more than just a worker in the fields. Even if it's just a degree from a technical school, it's still something you have to show for. At least you have an associate degree and a better chance to get a job with more long-term security. I consider myself successful and I am happy, but I am not close to where I eventually want to be. I am not done yet. (BM, 709–729)

During one of her interviews with a leading financial institution, they gave her a tour of the facility. They showed her the office she would have if this company hired her. She said she immediately thought of her parents.

> I thought of how proud they would be to see me in this office. I wanted them to see it and to introduce them to everybody. I am very proud of my parents. I am who I am because of them. (BM, 738–739)

Belinda talked about her future. We asked her where or how she saw herself in ten years. She did not talk much about her future professionally. Perhaps it is because she knows that that part of her life is a given. Ten years from now, Belinda sees herself with a home and well established.

> Personally, I want to have a family because I want to give my kids all those things I didn't have. I want my daughters to have piano lessons,

dancing lessons, all those things I always wanted but never had. I wanted to be in the band so badly. I realize that education makes all this possible. It will be easier for me than my parents. They worried about basic needs for us, but they provided more than enough. They gave us an opportunity and that's all we could ever ask for. Many children do not have those chances from the beginning. (BM, 748–759)

All her life she had been told that the only way to get a good job was to get a good education. She was excited and anxious to get out and find her dream job. Like most recent college graduates, Belinda suddenly realized that it was not going to be easy to find employment. She moved to San Antonio with her brother while she applied and interviewed for several jobs. She turned down a position in management with a major telephone company, and another offer from a title company. She was frustrated and disillusioned because she could not find something she really liked. She considered going to graduate school, but she felt she needed to work in order to help her parents. She also thought about teaching, but that would require her to go back to school for certification.

Belinda needed to work and could not wait much longer. She finally had to accept a job as a credit manager at a bank. However, she continued to consider other offers. She went through four screenings and several tests, and was one of 16 finalists with American National. She was the youngest of three females and the only recent college graduate in the group. All the others were males in their 30's and 40's, according to Belinda. Belinda was offered a job pending licensure as a financial consultant. She thought this was a great opportunity for her.

This is the kind of job I have been looking for because it gives me flexibility. The harder I work, the more money I can earn. I have never been scared of hard work so I know I will do very well. (BM, 778–782)

To conclude Belinda's story, we think it is only appropriate to describe her using the words of the most influential teacher she ever had. The teacher who helped her discover herself—Mr. G., her science teacher, coach, and friend. According to him she was unrelenting, persistent, determined, driven, adaptable, dramatic, simple, unselfish, and invincible. He described Belinda as

> a highly intelligent individual who has always been successful academ-ically and personally. Belinda has what Carl Rogers calls presence. When she walks into a room, she tends to dominate, or she tends to get everyone's attention. She doesn't demand it, but when she speaks, she does it with authority. She never gave up at anything she under-took. She was always monitoring and adapting. She believed in herself, and she always worked real hard. Even though people laughed at her because of the way she dressed or spoke, she didn't let it get her down. She knew they were laughing. I can't pinpoint the time or the day, but I remember she would keep up with the best kids and I know she had to work twice as hard sometimes. I'll never forget what she said. To this day it brings goose bumps to me. I remember her words, she said, "Sir, some day I'm going to be somebody." And I looked at her straight in the eye, and she was looking at me dead cold. Some-how I knew that this kid was not going to back down. She always tried so hard. She was the kind of kid that always went way beyond. She wanted to make sure that she didn't misunderstand. A lot of times she did not trust herself. I think in my class she felt she was given a fair chance, and she was given credit for it. She began to glow and she would just do more. She wanted to achieve. It was her incredible drive. She would stumble, but she wouldn't fall. She was invincible in the sense that she knew her strengths and used them to the maximum. She was very aware of her weaknesses also and worked on them con-stantly. That made her even stronger. She just felt so comfortable, and she was so confident inside. She actually thought she could take on the world. And for a while, I mean, even now, she probably can. (RG, 114–135)

Benito

"No one would have imagined I would be who I am today."

Benito, now a mayor and a lawyer, is known to be a very caring, giving, and unselfish person.

In retrospect, Benito now realizes how extraordinary his life journey has been.

> When I was growing up I didn't know any better. I didn't know I was poor. I thought everyone lived that way. As I got older I knew I was different, but I didn't think it was such a difficult life. Now I realize how amazing my life has been. (BG, 588–592)

We asked Benito why he thought he was so successful. Without hesitation he said, "First of all I feel I've been blessed, second was the tremendous family support, and third it was my teachers and coaches" (BG, 610–615).

He believes that most people who had to overcome tremendous odds probably have similar support systems.

> I think a big part is the upbringing. I think the basic values we learn at home are important. If you look at all the successful people, they all shared pretty much the same qualities. They had discipline at home, and parents taught them just basic moral principles. Basic things like what's right, what's wrong, work hard, don't cheat, and be fair. If you get taught those at home, you realize that everything else just sort of falls in place. If you have these core beliefs when you go to school your chances are enhanced. Some teachers are so good that they can identify and know how to touch that nerve to get some of those kids. The experience at home, coupled with a teacher that has that skill and heart to bring out the best in children is the best formula for success for all students. Teachers who are sensitive and see things from the student's eyes make the difference for success and failure for many children. (BG, 620–636)

Benito and his partner have established a very successful law practice. He is involved with several legal associations as a way to keep current. He now serves as the Chair of the Board of Directors for the Texas Young Lawyers Association. What makes this unique is that he is the first Hispanic to serve as the chairperson for this association. Benito invited us to one of his meetings at the Texas Law Center in Austin. We observed him as he ran the meeting much the same way he runs the city council meetings. Benito sat at the head of the table directing the meeting and he moved quickly and smoothly through the agenda. There were eight members present, four women and four men. The members participating the most were both minority representatives.

We also interviewed other people in the business community. We talked to a successful businesswoman who is actively involved in several organizations such as the Chamber of Commerce and the Rotary Club. Rosío is very pleased with the job Benito is doing. The thing that impresses her the most is Benito's trustworthiness. She feels that he is not the typical politician because he is not aligned with any groups or factions. "He does what he does because he genuinely cares about doing the right things for people" (RG, 4–8). According to her, the city has undergone many positive changes since incorporation and especially since Benito became mayor.

We also spoke to one of Benito's secretaries. Ann Marie provided some valuable information and validated most of what everyone else said about Benito. She had nothing but praise for Benito. She says some people do not know how much Benito does for the city. He puts in long hours and uses his law office and own resources to do lots of work at no cost. When we asked her what adjectives best describe him, she said that he was a very caring, giving, and unselfish person. She described him as a very dedicated, humble, sensitive, ethical, and honest person. She said he is "intelligent, driven, never stops, a hard worker, and always wants to make things better for people" (AM, 24–28). Though he runs a very successful law practice, he helps many poor people for free. "He is just such a caring person. Everything he does, he does it from his heart" (AM, 32–36).

Benito is involved in the schools as a volunteer, and teachers often invite him to speak to their students about success. He does not like to talk about success because he focuses more on helping children believe in themselves. He dedicates most of his time talking to children who are not doing well in school. His experience has been that most teachers who serve these students have low expectations. Many of these teachers start apologizing before he even speaks to their students. Benito says he knows better because "once I start sharing my story they are attentive and courteous to me" (BG, 640–647).

He said the real issue with these children is self-esteem: "We need to find a way to make them feel good about themselves. You just don't know who is going to be that person who touches you and makes a difference in your life" (BG, 656–658).

Benito's Views of Success and Reflection

Benito defined success several ways. He felt that most people who grow up poor tend to measure success materialistically. Benito is not different. The first definition he offered was:

> To me success is being able to do what you want to do and enjoying it. Before I became a lawyer, I dreamed of being able to walk into a store to buy a pair of pants or a shirt, and not have to worry about how much it cost. Success is just really being happy with yourself, and your job. A person who is successful is someone who is hard working, patient, and at peace within himself or herself. (BG, 344–350)

Like Sonia and Belinda, when people told Benito he was not capable, he was more determined to prove them wrong.

> When people tell me, you don't have the money, or *¿como le vas a hacer?* [how are you going to do it]? Those things tend to inspire some people and I'm one of those people who *me pongo más terco* [I get more stubborn]. I'm going to show them because I don't like to lose. (BG, 350–357)

Most people who know Benito think he is highly intelligent, but he does not think he is. To him intelligence is not an indicator of success. "By intelligence, I sort of mean education as well. I know very successful people who are not educated" (BG, 670–674). He says he is not intelligent, but he makes up for it by working hard and being persistent. "If it's something that's worth fighting for and it's important, I will fight you to the death. I will overwork you" (BG, 424–430).

Benito was confident he could do almost anything he sets out to do. He was never satisfied because he believed he could always do better. It was difficult for Benito to talk about himself.

> I think most people would think that I'm successful. Having my background, and being able to just graduate from high school could

be considered a big success. I was not necessarily in the honors class, but I graduated. It got more amazing, as I got older . . . going to college and graduating. Then it was going to law school, which seems incredible. And it doesn't stop there, eventually becoming not just another lawyer, but a good lawyer. Now I'm the mayor of my hometown. No one would have imagined I would be who I am today. I think it has been a pretty interesting journey for me. I'll be honest with you, the reason I'm having problems with these questions is because I've never really sat down and sort of looked back to think. What does it mean? Or what do people think? It's been going so fast that I've never had time to really stop this momentum. Participating in the study has forced me to look backwards. It's the first time that I've actually done some reflective kinds of things and tried to verbalize it. But I think overall, if I died tomorrow, I'd feel that I'd given it my best shot. (BG, 710–720)

Sonia

"School will be easier than working in the fields."

Sonia did not say much about her parents not being at her graduation. She knew that if she chose to stay they would not be there. It was indeed a celebration. The graduates were dressed in maroon and white gowns. The procession took forever. They were all sitting in the middle of the field, and we could not find Sonia in the crowd. The dignitaries were introduced, the top graduates were recognized, and the salutatorian and the valedictorian delivered their speeches. The principal certified the graduates, and the superintendent congratulated the students and their parents. Finally, the graduates walked one by one as their names were called to receive their diplomas. Sonia is "just another average student" lost in the crowd. She goes unnoticed, once again, like most of the 600–plus graduates. She will persevere like she always has done in her own quiet and inconspicuous way.

I don't think they will come 'cause once you start working, it's every day. No Sundays off. No, nothing. It's every day, every day for two months. So, they're not going to have time. I feel kind of sad, but then it's like they're working so, I'm just hoping that my sister can come down. I felt okay until senior mass. They played the song "Because You Love Me" by Céline Dion. All of us seniors had a rose that we were supposed to give our parents when the song was over. Instead, I gave the rose to my brother David and his wife. It made me sad, and I missed my parents. (SR, 743–755)

After the procession, we rushed down to the field to find Sonia. We were lucky to find her quickly. She seemed very happy. We hugged her and congratulated her one more time. We knew she was looking for her sister, brother, and her friends. We said goodbye so she could find them. We told her we would call and visit again soon.

When her parents left in April, Sonia thought she and her brother José would ride a bus to Washington after graduation to join them. However, José enrolled in summer classes at the university and they decided to stay. For the first time in her life, Sonia was at home for the summer. She was not picking asparagus, berries, or cucumbers this summer. She worked with a company doing inventory while she waited to come to Austin in the fall.

Sonia's dream had always been to attend St. Edward's University like her sister. "I plan to go to St. Ed's in Austin in the fall of 1997. My sister went there, and my cousins have been there. I don't want to stay in the Valley. . . .I want to move" (SR, 766–768).

When we talked to her in April she did not have her admission results yet. She seemed sure she would be accepted. We asked if anyone from school had helped her with the application process. She replied, "No, it was in College Night at school. [St. Edward's] came down and I got an application. I filled it out and I mailed it. It was just a simple application" (SR, 789–792).

She was notified in May that she had been accepted.

St. Edward's University is a four year, Catholic, independent, Liberal Arts university located in Austin, Texas. In 1972, St. Edward's University developed and hosted the first College Assistance Migrant Program (CAMP) in the nation. The purpose of this program is to offer an educational opportunity to the sons and daughters of migrant and seasonal farm workers. It is a freshman-level scholarship program funded by the U.S. Department of Education and St. Edward's University. Since its inception, St. Edward's has assisted more than 1,800 migrant students.

Each year, 40 students are chosen to participate. To qualify, students must provide information about the family's employment history. A student will be eligible only if he or she is a high school graduate or has attained a GED, meets St. Edward's admission requirements, and has parents who have been employed in migrant or seasonal farm work for at least 75 days in the 24 months prior to the date of application.

During the freshman year, each participant is awarded an average of $13,000 in financial assistance to cover tuition, books and supplies, room and board, transportation, health insurance, and a monthly stipend. Upon admission, CAMP students are expected to attend a weeklong orientation program. When they are enrolled, they meet with academic advisors biweekly, and attend a minimum of three tutoring and counseling sessions every week.

Sonia's Views of Success and Reflection

Sonia was not the valedictorian of her class. She was not an honor graduate or even in the top 25% of her class. She did not apply to MIT, Harvard, The University of Texas, or any other prestigious institution. She was not recruited or invited to visit any universities. Sonia was not awarded any scholarships. She did not even know she had to apply in order to receive one. This has not changed much since we, the authors, graduated. We sat on the edges of our seats expecting to receive various scholarships, such as the Spanish Club one. We later found out that we had to submit an application. We were also "average students" lost in the crowd.

Sonia was "just an average student," as she described herself. She was an average student as judged by the system. An average student according to the standards established for mainstream America, standards based on grade point averages and standardized test scores (SAT and ACT). As an "average student" she had to fend for herself, and she did it well. Her story tells us that she is far from average. She is one of very few migrant farm workers that make it through high school and one of 40 migrant students accepted to the CAMP program at St. Edward's University. Sonia is confident she will succeed. School will be easier than working in the fields.

Destiny's Architect

In order to survive their migratory ordeals, these three students had a set of special characteristics that helped them cope with very unfortunate and difficult circumstances. They were at the same time strong and gentle, tough and sensitive, proud and humble, cooperative and rebellious, shy and bold. They were extraordinarily unselfish in some ways, and yet extraordinarily self-centered in other ways. These seeming contradictions were symptomatic of their success.

Sonia, Belinda, and Benito shared many of the same personal characteristics such as, but not limited to, determination, persistence, a strong work ethic, responsibility, commitment, resourcefulness, and cooperation. However, one particular coping strategy was most conspicuous because all three participants specifically identified it. Their way of dealing with the persistent doubts of their capabilities by others was interesting. When their ability was questioned, they became more determined to overcome the obstacles placed before them. They refused to be discouraged or convinced that they were not capable. They channeled and managed their anger and other emotions in positive and effective ways to prove their nay-sayers wrong. This was their way of dealing with the debilitating low expectations of their teachers and the pervasive deficit thinking of the school system as a whole.

Belinda called it winning, Benito called it inspiration, and Sonia called it *coraje* (anger).

Belinda: "I could do anything I really wanted to do"

Eighth grade turned out to be a great year for Belinda. That's when she started participating in literary competitions. She prepared for two events, impromptu speaking and spelling.

> I was in spelling and impromptu speaking. There was a conflict in schedules with these two events for the district meet. I remember both of my coaches were arguing because both of them wanted me. I was there just watching them discuss it. I ended up doing impromptu, and had to miss out on spelling. I am so glad I chose impromptu. That was the turning point of my life. I remember after I won the district championship, I couldn't wait for the next day. I couldn't wait to come to school. The principal was going to announce the results, and that's when we had the awards assembly. After we got out of the assembly everybody was just congratulating me. It felt so good. That's when I was convinced I could do anything I really wanted to do. (BM, 180–194)

Belinda enjoyed high school and made the most of it. Mr. G. offered a simple explanation:

By the time she got to ninth grade she refused to take no for an answer. When she got to high school she already knew that she had rights, and she demanded equal treatment. She knew that she could be an honor student. She didn't want to be treated special, but she wanted to be treated just the same as everybody else. She sort of reached a mini-level of self-actualization. She came to realize who she was and how important she was. And I think she became a fighter for the underdog. She was trying to prove that we were all the same. (RG, 96–107)

Benito: "I'm going to show them because I don't like to lose"

Benito was an only child, raised by a widowed mother who dedicated her life to her son. She was poor in the sense of having material things, but rich with hope combined with high, non-negotiable aspirations for her son. She was determined to provide the best access to opportunities, and that was all Benito really needed, as illustrated in his amazing life story. Though confronted with many obstacles and the pervasive low expectations of the school system, Benito believed that he had control over his success or failure at school. He always knew he could do better than others expected. He was relentless in his efforts to get into the more challenging classes with the "better" teachers. To Benito, it was very personal when his ability was questioned. These doubts imposed on him by others raised his level of determination and persistence to succeed. No matter how difficult the challenges, Benito refused to be discouraged. He was resourceful and found ways to get things done. This resolve was evident with his attitude towards playing football.

> That was the one thing I had no doubt about. I knew I could do as well as anyone else. No matter what, I could block anybody. The ones that were my size or smaller I could over power. The ones that were bigger I could out speed because I was very fast, and the ones that were faster and stronger I would outsmart them with decoy blocking and other techniques. (BG, 37)

His approach to overcoming the obstacles and barriers placed before him by the school system and society in general, was similar to the approach he used on the football field.

Sonia: "I'll show you I can make it, and I will"

Sona's life was far from ordinary. It was clear that she had to overcome many factors other students could never even begin to imagine, much less encounter. Sonia had a way of turning negatives into positives. When she was confronted with obstacles and barriers, she overcame them with her positive attitude. She developed this coping strategy by living through a lifetime of challenges and struggle—challenges that made her strong and resilient.

She almost never mentioned any negative experiences, and had nothing bad to say about anyone. When we asked her if she thought she would make it in college, she said,

> Well, if you told me that I can't do it or you told me that no, I'll never make it, I fill up with *coraje* [anger]. Well, I'll show you I can make it. And I will....This is just school. I like school. I don't like working in the fields . . . it is much harder, and I've been able to do that all my life. (SR, 305–308, 310–313)

Sonia took us to her government/economics class. We observed her interact with her classmates as we talked to her teacher, Mr. Pose. His description of Sonia was very similar and consistent with the opinion of other people who knew her.

> Sonia is very smart, well organized, goal-oriented, and focused. She is shy but will speak out when she has to. She is disciplined, determined, and will do whatever it takes to get the work done. Her life experiences have made her strong. School will be easy for her compared to what she has lived through already. She is proud of who she is. (SR, 533–537)

Mr. Ríos was Sonia's computer/Co-op teacher. Sonia liked him because "he was very understanding and very patient with me. He was always encouraging us to do our best" (SR, 520–522). When we interviewed Mr. Ríos, he had nothing but praise and admiration for Sonia. He was very confident that Sonia would be successful in college and anything else she undertook because "she has extraordinary resolve and self-discipline. She is hardworking and never complains about anything in spite of her arthritic condition" (Mr. R, 67–69).

We met with three of her close friends and classmates. They were very articulate and helpful. Though their impression of Sonia was analogous to those of her teachers, their perceptions seemed less generic. They saw her through different lenses. They spoke as peers speak of friends. They spoke of her as someone other than a student. "Sonia is trustworthy. She expects the same things from herself that she expects from her friends. She knows what she wants to accomplish. She is very proud of who she is" (PNF, 79–82). There was a strong sense of admiration amongst her friends as they spoke of her accomplishments and her potential and determination to succeed.

These migrant students learned to like, appreciate, and love themselves by looking at themselves in the loving mirrors of their parents' eyes. They possessed deep optimism guided by internal values and standards. To resist their ordeals they needed self-esteem. Self-esteem determined how much they learned after something went wrong. It allowed them to receive praise and compliments. It acted as a buffer against hurtful statements while allowing receptivity to constructive criticism. Self-confidence was their reputation with themselves, how they thought of themselves. It allowed them to take risks without waiting for approval or reassurance from others. They expected to handle new situations well because of their past successes.

No one would have imagined that, against all odds, they would be who they are today.

VIII
ANALYSIS OF CENTRAL RESEARCH QUESTIONS

⊹

WE USED THE THEORY/NOTION OF ACADEMIC INVULNERABILITY (ALVA & PA-dilla, 1995) as a framework for cross-case analysis. The attrition rates among the Hispanic student population have been phenomenal and re-searchers have identified factors that contribute to their failure. Several studies have documented that Mexican American students are more likely to drop out of school than the general population (Brown, Rosen, Hill, & Olivas, 1980; Hirano-Nakanishi, 1986; National Commission on Sec-ondary Education for Hispanics, 1984; National Council of La Raza, 1992; Rumberger, 1983; Valverde, 1987). The National Center for Ed-ucational Statistics (1989) has estimated that national dropout rates stand at 36% for Hispanics, 15% for Blacks, and 13% for Whites.

The research clearly has illustrated the facts and causes for the high failure rates of this special population. Studies have been thorough in identifying the sociocultural factors that condemn these children to fail-ure. These studies have linked the poor achievement of Hispanic children to a number of sociocultural variables such as the educational and occu-pational attainment levels of parents, family income and composition, ethnic and language minority status, and the absence of learning materi-als in the home. The assumption is generally held that these sociocultural variables are the cause of the disproportionately high level of academic failure and attrition prevalent among Hispanic students (Arias, 1986; Rumberger, 1983, 1987; Steinberg, Blinde, & Chan, 1984).

Although many studies have identified numerous demographic factors that predispose Hispanic students to failure in school, not much is known about students who have survived the impeding effects of these sociocultural disadvantages. Educators and policymakers have long known about the severity of academic underachievement of Hispanic children, but very little is known about the factors and processes that influence and mediate this problem. Little attention has been given to students who overcome a number of socioeconomic and cultural disadvantages to succeed academically. Little is known about the academically successful Hispanic student and what distinguishes that student from those who experience academic failure. Alva and Padilla (1995) referred to these children as the "academically invulnerable" students in schools. Why do some students succeed while others fail despite sharing similar socioeconomic and cultural backgrounds?

We use the notion of academic invulnerability as a heuristic tool to examine academic achievement among the Hispanic student population holistically. The conceptual framework presented by Alva and Padilla (1995) is useful for testing an interactive approach for the study of Hispanic academic performance. This model consists of three factors. It facilitates looking at the overall dynamics and interaction between sociocultural, personal, and environmental factors and how this interaction influences the cognitive appraisal that students have of the schooling process as well as outcome measures of academic performance. The model focuses on the personal and environmental resources on which Hispanic students rely to meet educational challenges and opportunities. The academically invulnerable student develops many coping strategies that are manifested in the form of personal characteristics. The key characteristics are: determination, persistence, a strong work ethic, responsibility, commitment, resourcefulness, cooperation, a sense of hope, and several others. To understand the phenomenon of "academic invulnerability," the model calls for a multivariate assessment of these factors in the study of academic achievement of Mexican American students.

Alva and Padilla (1995) suggested that Hispanic students who succeed overcome psychosocial stress factors (socio-cultural variables) associated with their lifestyle and culture. They develop protective resources (personal and environmental) that make them invulnerable. Students "at-risk" who succeed possess a multitude of coping strategies that make them resilient to the stressful factors of acculturation (Garmezy, 1983, 1991).

The themes that emerged in this study are consistent and congruent with the description of invulnerable and resilient children. Five major themes emerged from the three cases: (a) stressors (sociocultural factors), (b) personal characteristics (personal resources), (c) support (environmental resources), (d) expectations and caring, and (e) coping strategies. To analyze the data across the three case studies, this analysis section is divided into the five themes.

Related Themes

Research has suggested that the conflict between the cultural values of Hispanic children and those required by the educational system is primarily responsible for the problems that Hispanic children have experienced in the classroom (Alva & Padilla, 1995). This research has implied that Hispanic children lack the competencies, values, and personality characteristics to help them succeed in school. According to this interpretation, in order to succeed, Hispanic children must adapt to the school environment through acculturation. Although acculturation may facilitate success, the process can be difficult and stressful. As children try to find their place within a new culture, they also struggle to create an identity that combines their experiences with the expectations of the new culture (Padilla, 1980, 1986). Cárdenas and Cárdenas (1977) referred to this cultural mismatch as incompatibility. Their model, the *theory of incompatibilities*, is a tested belief that the failure of minority children can be attributed to a lack of compatibility between their characteristics and the characteristics of a typical instructional program. "An instructional program developed for a white, Anglo-Saxon, English-speaking middle-class school population cannot be adequate for a non-white, non-Anglo-Saxon, non-English-speaking or non-middle-class population" (Cárdenas & Cárdenas, p. 1). Cárdenas and Cárdenas identified over 40 incompatibilities between the school system and Hispanic migrant children and grouped them into five categories: poverty, culture, language, mobility, and societal perceptions.

There is a deep-seated cultural belief in schools that education is a competition, a race. When education is viewed as a competition, the values of hard work, effort, and winning are glorified. Unfortunately, when this metaphor is invoked, something is left out. In this case, it is the losers. Education in the United States has been organized as a competition for precious resources. Gifted programs in elementary school lead to honors programs in high schools and admission to elite colleges and universities. This competitive system, with fewer slots at higher levels, requires a certain amount of failure (McDermott, 1989).

In contrast, Hispanic migrant students grow up in homes where it is important to work as a family. They spend months working alongside their parents, traveling from place to place, and living in crowded conditions. It is not surprising that their learning style is one of cooperation and collaboration.

In a study of cooperative versus competitive behaviors of Anglo, Black, Mexican American, and Mexican National elementary school children (Madsen & Shapira, 1970), the results showed Anglo and Black students were more competitive than Mexican American and Mexican students. Kagan and Madsen (1971) conducted an experiment involving learning activities with Mexican National, Mexican American, and Anglo children. The first controlled activity was based on typical middle-class Anglo competition, and the Anglo children outperformed the Mexican American children, who in turn outperformed the Mexican children. The researchers conducted a second learning activity, but based it on cooperation rather than competition. The Mexican children outperformed the Mexican American children, and both outperformed the Anglo children.

There is little doubt that children who learn to learn within one culture and then must learn in the modes of another experience confusion and dislocation in the process. They encounter different values considered essential for learning, and they are suddenly penalized or rejected for behaviors they have been taught to follow at home (e.g., not asking questions, no eye contact, not attempting to do what they are not sure of being able to do successfully). Different cultures prefer different child-rearing practices that have significant effects on later learning (Saville-Troike, 1978). Many children also face communication problems because they speak a language other than English. The learning of culture, like the learning of language, begins with children's first experiences with the family into which they are born, the community to which they belong, and the environment in which they live. By the time they come to school at the age of 5 or 6, they have already internalized many of the basic values and beliefs of their native culture. They have also learned the rules of behavior that are considered appropriate for their role in the community and have established the procedures for continued socialization. They have learned how to learn.

Stressors: Sociocultural Factors

The poor academic achievement of Hispanic students has been linked to a number of sociocultural variables. Among the sociocultural factors associated with their school performance are: (a) mobility, (b) poverty, (c) ethnic and language minority status, (d) children's need to work, (e) family income and composition, (f) educational level and occupational status of their parents, (g) substandard housing, and (h) the absence of learning materials in the home.

Coupled with the at-risk variables affecting Hispanic students in general, migrant children's lives are affected by many other factors related to their lifestyle. Their unique conditions make them more intensely at risk than the general Hispanic population. The two main factors that impact migrant children are mobility and poverty. They are among the poorest and most impoverished children in American schools (Shotland, 1989). In addition to the problems associated with mobility and poverty, another impeding factor is the need to work or care for younger children (Chavkin, 1991). These children face many other hardships associated with their migrant lifestyle. They live in deplorable substandard housing as they travel from place to place in search of work.

Yet, in spite of all these seemingly insurmountable obstacles, not all migrant children experience failure in school. Sonia, Belinda, and Benito, the three participants in this study, serve as examples of at-risk students who defied the odds. They persevered and succeeded in a system not designed for them. Their ability to overcome barriers depended on their personal resources (attitudes, skills, and knowledge) and the environmental resources in place to provide support (Alva & Padilla, 1995).

The three participants suffered but overcame the extreme life event stressors associated with their lifestyle. They struggled through severe and adverse conditions prompted by the general sociocultural variables of their culture and the unique, risk factors of their migrant lifestyle.

Mobility

When migrant workers move around in search of work, they may consider factors such as the availability of different school systems, curricula, social conditions, and late starts or early exits during the school year.

Problems with records and credit transfers are migration-related problems that contribute to lower academic achievement and high dropout rates among migrant students (Cox et al., 1992). The frequent change of environment keeps the migrant child in a continuous state of adjustment to school, friends, and language. Constant mobility makes it hard for farm worker children to complete their education. These students average two to three schools a year and are usually behind grade level by 6– 18 months (Harrington, 1987).

In our study, Sonia, the youngest participant, was the most active migrant of the three. She made the trip to Washington every summer for 17 years. Belinda started when she was in the second grade and quit when she was a sophomore. Benito had worked in the fields since he was very young, but his migrant experience did not begin until he was in the fifth grade. He and his mother migrated until he was in the ninth grade.

Poverty

Several studies (Barrington & Hendricks, 1989; Laosa, 1982; Rosenthal, Milne, Ellman, Ginsburg, & Baker, 1983; Rumberger, 1983; Steinberg et al., 1984) have indicated that students from economically disadvantaged families are more likely to be retained in school or drop out than those from more economically stable families. According to a 1992 study, about two-thirds of migrant students come from families where earnings are below the poverty level (Strang et al., 1993). The cost of migrating can be high. Very often migrant families arrive at their new destinations with little or no money for food or housing (Prewitt-Díaz et al., 1989). Many migrant students suffer educational disadvantages related to poverty and poverty-related health problems, which can have a direct effect educational performance (Huang, 1993).

Benito and his mother were the poorest of the three families we interviewed. He and his mother lived on $40 a month from social security and food stamps. Sonia's and Belinda's families earned reasonable money during the summers once all the children were old enough to work. Nevertheless, individually, their hourly wages were considerably less than minimum wage. In most cases, the families borrowed money to make the trip north to work.

Ethnic and Language Minority Status

About 80% of migrant students come from Latino backgrounds, and as many as 90% of migrant students come from homes where a language other than English is spoken. Approximately one-third of these students were born outside the United States. Many of these students and their parents have had little or no formal schooling in their native country (Cox et al., 1992). Many Mexican American families depend on their children to serve as interpreters of a new language and culture. As their children learn English and become familiar with the new cultural environment, they are needed to interpret or translate for their parents. As a result, their children become involved in the financial, legal, and social worries and concerns of the family (Szapocznik, Kurtines, & Hanna, 1979).

Our three participants are first-generation immigrants from México. The participants were born in the United States, but all three families initially came to the United States illegally. Their parents did not speak or write English and could not help them much with their schoolwork. As they grew older and learned to speak English, they all served as interpreters for their parents and family.

Children's Need to Work

Migrant children are always expected to work in the fields or to care for younger brothers and sisters while their parents are at work (Chavkin, 1991). Young migrant children can make a significant contribution to their family's income by working rather than attending school (Prewitt-Díaz et al., 1989). Consequently, education becomes a secondary priority. This results in an increased level of absenteeism and contributes to low graduation rates. Working in the fields exposes migrant students to a variety of health risks from accidental injury or exposure to pesticides.

Sonia, Belinda, and Benito all helped their parents in the fields even when they were not old enough to earn wages. Their parents had no choice because there was nowhere else to leave them when they left for the fields early in the mornings. The children helped any way they could, by picking onions, melons, strawberries, or asparagus, or counting sacks and baskets. Each family needed all the children to work in order to make their trips worthwhile.

Family Income and Composition

The annual wages for the majority of these workers is less than $7,500 (Effland, Hamm, & Oliveira, 1993). The average income for a migrant family of 5.3 members was about $5,500 in 1988 (De Mers, 1988).

As migrant farm workers, all three families were under the poverty level. Sonia and Belinda come from large families. Sonia is the youngest of six children; Belinda is the fifth of six. On the other hand, Benito's mother raised him as an only child.

Educational and Occupational Status

Educational backgrounds and status vary among migrant groups. Hispanic migrants who have lived in the United States for generations have some knowledge of English, whereas many recent arrivals are not literate in any language. For some, this condition is a result of their social and economic status. For others, illiteracy results from disruption of education caused by frequent moves or political turmoil (Wallace, 1986).

High mobility impacts student achievement, especially when it is coupled with poverty and living in uneducated, illiterate families. The median educational level for the head of a migrant family was 6 years in 1986 (Harrington, 1987). The educational level of the parents of the participants in this study varies slightly but not significantly. Both of Belinda's parents and Sonia's mother finished *primaria* (sixth grade) in México. Sonia's father was in and out of schools in the United States but never long enough to be promoted to the next grade. Benito's mother never went to school.

There is a strong relationship between occupational and educational status. Finding and keeping employment is the greatest challenge for parents, particularly fathers and male members of the family (Valdez, 1996). The occupational history of the parents in this study supports this correlation. Except for Benito's mother, their primary occupations have always been farm work. Sonia's and Belinda's parents became migrant farmworkers immediately upon their arrival to this country. Benito and his mother joined the migrant stream later. Sonia's parents still travel to Washington and Oregon every year.

Substandard Housing

Housing conditions vary greatly from area to area and camp to camp. Some migrants live in well-kept labor camps or houses furnished by the growers or state or federal agencies. At the other extreme, some migrant families have had to live in barns, sheds, orchards, in their cars and trucks or under bridges (Prewitt-Díaz et al., 1989). In general, migrant farmworkers average 191 days of farm work a year. Migrant families are forced to live in substandard housing that provides minimal or no cooking accommodations or other appliances. The lack of refrigeration makes it impossible to keep meat or milk, essential elements for the healthy growth of children, who are often the most severely affected by the migratory lifestyle (Whitener, 1985).

For Sonia, Belinda, and Benito, housing conditions were almost always deplorable everywhere they went. They were crowded and in general, lacked basic amenities. For Sonia and Belinda, adapting to these living conditions was especially difficult because they lived in comfortable homes back in Texas.

Absence of Learning Materials

The lack of financial resources made it difficult for the participants' parents to provide instructional materials at home. They spent most of their earnings on clothes and school supplies for their children when they came back to Texas each fall. The parents always provided their children with essential school materials such as paper, pencils, crayons, and backpacks. However, they did not have access to encyclopedias, books, computers, and other learning materials for their homes.

Personal Characteristics: Personal Resources

It is not difficult to understand how the stressful effects connected to risk factors may create a sense of failure and hopelessness for many students. What is difficult to explain is how the migratory lifestyle that supposedly dooms these children to fail may also be the reason why many migrant children succeed. Risk factors impede success, but on the other hand, their way of life also facilitates experiences that help them develop personal resources that make them resilient. Children's lifestyles can be blamed for their academic failure, but they must also be given credit for their success. Students like Sonia, Belinda, and Benito survived the negative effects of these stressors because of lessons learned as members of a migrant farm worker family.

Sonia, Belinda, and Benito share an extensive core of values and beliefs. This core includes determination, persistence, a strong work ethic, responsibility, commitment, resourcefulness, cooperation, and a sense of hope. The migrant experience was like a survival training session designed to help them develop the personal resources common to the resilient child. Their resilience, coupled with their intellectual potential, helped to mediate their reaction to stressful life events and conditions.

The concept of resilience has been used in other fields such as health and psychiatric research for a long time. It has generated considerable interest in understanding the characteristics that enable individuals to survive severe trauma. Resilience is an interaction between the characteristics of the individual and the environment. It is not an attribute; it is the way in which individuals modify their responses to risk situations and operate at turning points during their lives (Garmezy, 1991; Rutter, 1987). Garmezy (1983) and others have identified individual characteristics of resilient students. These characteristics include (a) positive peer and adult interactions; (b) low degrees of defensiveness and aggressiveness and high degrees of cooperation, participation, and emotional stability (based on teachers' ratings), (c) a positive sense of self, (d) a sense of personal power rather than powerlessness, and (e) an internal locus of control (a belief that they are capable of exercising a degree of control over their environment).

Resilient children also tend to have parents who value education, and the children know their parents are concerned about their schooling. Another important characteristic of resilient children is having at least one significant adult in their lives (Clark, 1983; Fine & Schwebel, 1991).

Sonia, Belinda, and Benito believed they had some control over their academic success or failure, and they felt good about their school performance in general. All three participants knew they could do better, and their goal was always to get into the more challenging classes. When their ability was questioned, they were more determined to prove they were capable.

Sonia

Participants' parents, family, teachers, and friends consistently identified many of the personal characteristics associated with resilience. Sonia has "exceptional ability, drive, and is very persistent. She just never gives up," according to Mr. Avalos, one of her teachers (Mr. A, 56). Though she suffers from juvenile rheumatoid arthritis, Mr. Ríos said, "She never complains, she always does her work and everything else that needs to get done. She has lots of ambition, a great attitude, and is definitely hardworking" (Mr. R, 25). He believes she will be successful in college because "she has extraordinary resolve and self-discipline. She is hardworking and never complains about anything in spite of her arthritic condition" (Mr. R, 67–69).

Sonia overcomes negatives with her positive attitude and determination. "Well, if you told me that I can't do it or you told me that no, I'll never make it, I fill up with *coraje* [anger]. Well, I'll show you I can make it. And I will" (SR, 305–308). Sonia's government teacher described her as follows:

> Sonia is very smart, well organized, goal oriented, and focused. She is shy but will speak out when she has to. She is disciplined, determined, and will do whatever it takes to get the work done. Her life experiences have made her strong. School will be easy for her compared to what she has lived through already. She is proud of who she is. (SR, 533–537)

Her sister said Sonia has "always had a good sense of direction, academically and socially. Sonia is very sensitive. She gets along with other people....She at times is very quiet and reserved, but she gets her work done . . . she's very dependable and hard working." According to her mother,

> *Todo el tiempo fue muy dedicada a sus estudios. Le gustaba mucho escribir y leer desde que estaba muy chica. Nosotros nunca tuvimos que decirle que hiciera sus tareas.* [She has always been dedicated to her studies. She liked to write and read since she was very little. We never had to tell her to do her homework.] (AR, 123–126)

Sonia is confident about herself. She is sure she will do well in college. She has developed coping strategies that have made her strong and resilient. When we asked her if she thought she would make it in college, she said: "This is just school. I like school. I don't like working in the fields...it is much harder, and I've been able to do that all my life" (SR, 310–313).

Belinda

Mr. and Mrs. Magallán depended on Belinda as their negotiator and interpreter.

> *Belinda no tenía vergüenza hablar con los patrones americanos . . . tenía mucha confianza en si misma y era como una abogada para nosotros.* [She was not shy when she spoke to the boss . . . she was self-confident and she was like a lawyer for us]. (MM, 23–24)

Her mother said, "*Belinda siempre ha tenido mucha ambición y empeño con sus estudios y con su trabajo.* [Belinda has always had ambition and dedication to her studies]" (MM, 25–26).

Mr. Garcia, an important teacher in her life, described Belinda as a highly intelligent student who has always been successful academically and personally. She was unrelenting, persistent, determined, driven, adaptable, dramatic, simple, unselfish, and invincible. "She wanted to achieve. It was her incredible drive. I'll never forget Belinda. She's was a go-getter, she was determined, she was a dreamer, and an achiever. Those are things I always noticed in her." Mr. Garcia was impressed with her extraordinary self-discipline and determination. He remembers her words clearly: "Sir, I'm going to win the district championship. I don't care how long we have to practice. I don't care what we have to do sir, I want to win" (RG, 240–243).

Belinda knows the journey has been difficult, but it is not over yet. "I consider myself successful and I am happy, but I am not close to where I eventually want to be. I am not done yet" (BM, 709–729). As a youngster she was ashamed of being a migrant. She was embarrassed that her parents did not speak English. She is now very proud of the way she grew up. "I started to feel proud of myself, my parents, my family, and our lifestyle. When I was getting ready to off to college, I realized what my parents meant to me and how much they cared about me" (BM, 731–742).

Benito

Benito's secretary described him as a caring, giving, and unselfish person.

> He is very dedicated, humble, sensitive, ethical, and honest. He is intelligent, driven, never stops, a hard worker, and always wants to make things better for people. He is just such a caring person. Everything he does, he does it from his heart.

His concern for people is evident. According to Rocío, a constituent, "He does what he does because he genuinely cares about doing the right things for people" (RG, 4–8). His mother feels Benito is a caring person. "*Mi hijo es muy bueno . . . si puede ayudarte, el te va ayudar de una manera.* [My son is a kind person . . . if he can help you, he will one way or another]" (NG, 112–114).

Benito does not see himself as intelligent, but he says he works hard and is very persistent. "If it's something that's worth fighting for and it's important, I will fight you to the death. I will over work you" (BG, 424–430). He believes he can do almost anything if he works hard at it. His close friends were amazed at his determination. "No matter what, he always tried hard and never used it [poverty] as an excuse. He was determined, dedicated, and driven. I knew he would make it because he has lots of heart" (GG, 5–7). No matter how difficult the challenges, Benito refused to be discouraged. He was resourceful and found ways to get things done. This resolve was evident with his attitude about life:

> Being able to just graduate from high school could be considered a big success. I was not necessarily in the honors class, but I graduated. It got more amazing as I got older. Going to college and graduating. Then it was going to law school, which seems incredible. And it doesn't stop there, eventually becoming not just another lawyer, but a good lawyer. Now I'm the mayor of my hometown. No one would have imagined I would be who I am today. I think it has been a pretty interesting journey for me. (BG, 710–720)

Support: Environmental Resources

A strong support system is a critical factor that mediates children's success or failure to adapt to their environment. This support system is manifested in the form of the environmental resources available to these children. "The concept of environmental resources refers to external sources of information, support, and affective feedback, which, when available, can affect how well children adapt to their environment" (Alva & Padilla, 1995, p. 4). The environmental resources children depend on can be traced to two main sources: their families and schools. Sonia, Belinda, and Benito attribute their success to the support they drew from their families and schools.

Family Support

Children depend on parents, grandparents, and siblings for constant and unconditional support. Children who are raised in supportive family environments show the benefits, both academically and socially.

Sonia. Sonia is convinced that the reason she has done fairly well in school is because of the strong sense of family unity and the support her parents have facilitated. She believes her family has been her primary support system and credits her family for her success. "My parents have helped me a lot. They've taught me that education is the only way for me to get along with my life. My parents have given me a lot of encouragement. They value education a lot" (SR, 251–263). Her parents did not want their children working in the fields all their lives like them. Mrs. Ramírez said,

> *Bueno, pues nosotros no queríamos que fueran como uno. Uno quería que los hijos fueran más arriba y que estudiaran. Queríamos que fueran a la escuela. Es un vida muy dura y es duro para uno ver que sus hijos sigan trabjando en la labor. Nos venimos a los Estados Unidos para darles una vida mejor a nuestros hijos.* [Well, we did not want them to be like us. We wanted them to do better and to study. We wanted them to go to school. It is a hard life, and it is hard for us to see our children working in the fields. We came to the United States to provide a better life for our children.] (AR, 67–74)

Sonia's parents have been an inspiration to her and the driving force in her life. She feels a strong sense of support and security from them.

> My Dad . . . well, my parents, both of them, they always put us first. Our education. Everything. Their children go first before them . . .

always put us first, or try to help us first, they are very supportive. Well, they've always been there for us. They've tried to help us whenever we've needed them. And they're nice. They've loving. They're caring. If my parents wouldn't care about education, I don't think I would have done as well. (SR, 98–115)

As the youngest in her family, she enjoyed the attention naturally given to the baby of the family, not only from her parents but her siblings as well.

I was kind of spoiled 'cause I was the baby, but only when I was smaller. Yeah, my sister and my brothers all of them helped me. What we've all gone through is the same. So we all, we all tell each other that we have to . . . that we have to finish school. That we have to keep going and keep studying. And, well, since I'm the youngest, everybody tells me. I get talked to a lot. (SR, 157–155).

The most influential person in Sonia's life was someone within her family. Her sister was her role model. She wanted to be like her or better. Sonia is determined to follow in her older sister's footsteps. She quickly admits that Ana was her role model.

Well, she's my sister and she has gone through college. She's done it on her own. She's been able to go through school and complete it and stuff. So she's successful right now. What she's wanted to do, she's accomplished it. I want to follow in her footsteps. Maybe even try to beat her. . . .I admire my sister, but I want to do better than her and surpass her accomplishments. (SR, 235–246)

Sonia's parents want her to continue her studies. They do not want her to go too far from home, but their support is evident. "*Nosotros estamos dispuestos a apoyarla para que siga estudiando y logre sus propósitos.* [We are willing to support her so she can keep studying and achieve her goals]" (AR, 144–145).

Belinda. Belinda's family support was most important during her early school years. Her parents provided the fundamental support that helped her develop personal protective resources. These resources were important as she struggled to endure the low expectations of the school system. As she got older, she persevered by being resourceful. Belinda developed relationships with supportive teachers, counselors, and other school staff; she learned to manipulate the system. She created opportunities to get involved and she did not accept being left out.

Her parents always encouraged and supported her the best way they could. Their goal was to get their children out of the migrant life cycle. They always made sure they returned to Texas before the first day of school in the fall. There was always enough work, and they needed the money, but they returned because *"lo primero eran los niños, no queríamos que faltaran a la escuela* [first it was the children, we did not want them to miss school]" (JM, 59–63). Belinda remembered it was important for her parents. "My parents made sure we were back by the first day of school. Even if there was still work, we would always come back. Other families would stay and go to other states also" (BM, 101–106).

Belinda believes her parents wanted the best for her, but they did not know her potential nor understand her dreams. She felt restricted by their expectations. Her parents valued education, but Belinda wondered why her parents did not expect more from her. "Your parents are supposed to be the ones who push you to do more. My parents would ask me why couldn't I be like my sister. They wanted me to go to a technical school and stay close to home" (BM, 215–222).

Benito. Benito's life revolved entirely around his mother. His mother dedicated her life to him. She provided incredible support in spite of stressful conditions. Benito and his mother were poor and alone, and that seemed to draw them close. Without his mother's extraordinary support, Benito would never have had the opportunity to embark on his amazing journey. His mother nurtured him and made him strong with her unending love. She took good care of him.

> No matter how poor we were, I was always clean. I remember I was still in bed when my mom would iron my clothes so they would be warm when I put them on. My clothes were worn out but clean and pressed all the time. (BG, 112–115)

She laid the foundation that helped him work through everyday life but also prepared him for the more difficult obstacles he would encounter as he grew older. There is little doubt that Benito prevailed against life's most difficult challenges because of his mother. He acknowledges and credits his mother for his success. Benito's relationship with his mother is remarkable as illustrated in the following quote:

> She is just embedded in everything that happens and that I do. All my life when I was growing up, it was just she and I. I knew everything she was doing, and she knew everything I was doing. I always knew where she was. . . .Well, she gave everything to me. . . .I can sense the bond between me and my mom is different than all my friends with their moms. It's stronger, it's different, and not because it's better, but simply because it was a different type of sacrifice, a different type of bond that's between us. (BG, 33–58)

Benito thinks he was successful because "first of all, I feel I've been blessed, second was the tremendous family support, and third it was my teachers and coaches" (BG, 610–615).

School Support

Schools are an important source of environmental resources for many students. In the schools, caring teachers, counselors, principals, and a positive school climate can minimize students' stressful adjustment to the school environment.

Sonia. Unlike Belinda and Benito, Sonia depended mostly on her parents and family for support. She did not identify any particular person in school who inspired or motivated her or made a difference in her life. However, she did not remember any significant negative experiences with any teachers, either. She went through school as an average student and got help and support when she needed it.

Belinda. Belinda was successful in school because she was determined, motivated, and intelligent. However, she had to turn to her teachers for support and encouragement. She believes the main reason why her parents did not insist that she stay close to home and go to a vocational school was because of Mr. G. and one of the authors. She told us,

> I remember you went to my house to talk to my parents. They couldn't believe what you were telling them about me. You told them I could be a doctor, *ella puede ser abogada puede ser lo que quiera* [she can be a lawyer, she can be whatever she wants]. My dad was amazed and asked,

"¿usted cree?" [you think so?]. It was then when they accepted that I was going to college and it didn't matter where. Mr. García and you were the main difference in my life. If it hadn't been for you two, I would just be a secretary. I would have gone to vocational school. (BM, 3–15)

When Belinda went to junior high, her life as a student began to transform. She was involved in two activities that would impact the rest of her life. First, she participated in and won the district championship in impromptu speaking. Second, she was one of 14 students who made presentations at state and national migrant conferences. She began to feel proud of herself and her lifestyle. She got exposure and recognition. Consequently, when she went to high school, she received support from her teachers unlike before. She remembers some of these experiences. Her self-confidence soared as teachers acknowledged and recognized her in their classrooms.

I remember in every class the teachers all said something when they saw me in their class. They recognized me in front of the class. They explained to the whole class who I was and what I did. They said they were very proud to have me in their class. That made me feel real good and very important. (BM, 255–260)

Belinda transferred her networking skills to college. She was confident she would earn her degree, but it was not easy. As in junior high and high school, she found someone she could to talk to.

I would always go to Dr. García when I was down or worried about something. He would encourage me. He would say, *"usted puede señorita Belinda, usted no se me achicopale, usted para delante* [you can do it Belinda, don't you get down on yourself, you go forward]." He kept me going when things were rough. (BM, 486–497)

Belinda had extraordinary potential for success, but she depended on environmental resources to succeed. Her parents supported her efforts while she developed the personal resources that would help her access support from school.

Benito. Besides his mother, other people in high school and college provided Benito the support his mother could not give him. Several coaches made a difference in Benito's life, but one in particular had the most influence on him. Coach Ponce took care of Benito and helped him in many ways. Benito acknowledges that he was the key person in his life other than his mother:

> He was the one person without question of all the coaches that was the main difference for me. He showed me discipline. I think encouragement has come along the way from several sources. But you know, when Coach Ponce did some of the things for me, I don't know why he did it. I don't think he did it because he was a coach. I think he did it more because he was a Christian. He did some things that most teachers don't do. Spending his own money, gas, his car, and his time to take me to college. Giving me advice like a father I never had. He turned my life around. I think the reason Oscar sort of gave me special attention was because he didn't have his dad either. He was raised by his mom. He had been raised very poor also. He used to tell me that he saw many similarities between us. I don't know whether he felt sorry for me, but he knew that I needed the help. He was there at that critical time when I was a teenager getting ready to graduate from high school. That was real important, and I think he's one of the key people that actually touched that nerve to open my eyes a little bit more. (BG, 37–43)

When Benito went to college, Dr. Bernal took Coach Ponce's place as Benito's mentor and advisor. He helped him believe in himself, and he urged him to go to law school.

Benito used his personal resources skillfully to access important environmental resources. His support system came primarily from the strong and meaningful relationships he established with important people in his life.

Expectations and Caring

The most vivid and clear expectations were always coming from the family, teachers and mentors.

Family Expectations

The high expectations of parents is a major factor that influences school performance of children. Sonia, Belinda, and Benito all acknowledge their parents for their success. Sonia: "If my parents wouldn't care about education, I don't think I would have done as well." Belinda: "I am very proud of my parents. I am who I am because of them." Benito: "All my life when I was growing up, it was just she and I. I knew everything she was doing, and she knew everything I was doing." Some at-risk children manage to be successful because of high parental expectations. The parents of all three participants had high educational expectations for all their children, though none had more than a sixth-grade education. Dropping out of high school was never an option for any of their children, and it was understood that they would pursue further studies or training after graduation. Children who live in families "characterized by warmth, support, and clear rules and expectations, have low rates of failure" (Benard, 1991, p. 9). The participants' families met these criteria for success. Their migrant lifestyle taught their children valuable lessons for survival, but they did not want their children toiling in the fields the rest of their lives.

Caring Families

A powerful predictor of success for children at risk is the quality caring within the family. It was evident that Sonia, Belinda, and Benito had parents and family that took exceptional care of them. Sonia: "My parents, both of them, they always put us first. They've tried to help us whenever we've needed them. And they're nice. They're loving." Belinda: "I started to feel proud of myself, my parents, my family, and our lifestyle. When I was getting ready to off to college, I realized what my parents meant to me and how much they cared about me." Benito: "As a kid I remember I didn't have fancy clothes but I was always clean, I was always ironed, dinner was always done when I got home, I always got breakfast before I left for school." Despite the overwhelming risk factors, most academically successful students establish a relationship with a person they can turn to for care and support (Benard, 1991). A caring and supportive relationship is a critical variable that impacts the lives of resilient children. Children need unconditional love and caring from significant others to alleviate the debilitating effects of stressful life events (Rutter, 1979, 1984).

School Expectations

Schools convey positive and high expectations to students in many ways. The most powerful is through the relationships established between teachers or other school staff and students (Howard, 1990; Werner & Smith, 1989). This was especially true for Sonia, Belinda, and Benito. The system as a whole did not expect much from them, but they all established relationships with individual teachers, coaches, and other school staff who believed in them. Sonia's high school teachers had no doubt she would go to college and be successful. Belinda could depend on Mr. G. and one of the authors for support and care, while Benito had Coach Ponce as his mentor. Children who are successful feel like they are respected and their strengths and abilities are acknowledged (Benard, 1991). Effective teachers look for their students' strengths and interests and build on them to enhance their learning. For Belinda, it was Mr. G., who saw "the gleam in her eyes" and helped her believe in herself. Benito received extraordinary recognition because of his athletic ability, but Coach Ponce set the expectations and supported him. In college, Dr. Bernal continued to provide guidance and support for him.

Besides high expectations, caring teachers also provide the necessary support to make sure that their students live up to these expectations (Benard, 1995). A climate of high expectations in schools is a critical factor in reducing academic failure. Challenging at-risk students with a more demanding accelerated curriculum produces more positive academic and social outcomes (Levin, 1988), whereas children who are tracked into low-ability classes tend to experience poor academic success (Oakes, 1985). For Sonia, her parents became the primary source of support. For Belinda, Mr. G. gave her the opportunity to experience success and realize her potential. In Benito's case, Coach Ponce cared for him as if he were his own son. Successful students usually have at least one person in their lives who has accepted them unconditionally (Werner & Smith, 1992). These three participants were no exception. They found teachers they could turn to who facilitated ways to help them meet their basic needs for social support, caring, and love. The level of caring and support within the school is a powerful predictor of positive outcomes for students. Outside the family circle, children's role models are very often teachers.

Coping Strategies

In order to succeed, the three participants developed many coping strategies that helped them overcome incredible physical and emotional circumstances. These strategies were manifested in several ways but were mostly illustrated in the form of personal characteristics such as determination, persistence, a strong work ethic, responsibility, commitment, resourcefulness, cooperation, and several others.

Sonia, Belinda, and Benito shared most of these personal characteristics. However, one particular coping strategy was considerably conspicuous—it was specifically identified by all three participants. Their way of dealing with the persistent doubts of their capabilities was interesting. When their ability was questioned, they became more determined to overcome the obstacles placed before them. They refused to be discouraged or convinced that they were not capable. They channeled and managed their anger and other emotions in positive and effective ways to prove their naysayers wrong. This was their way of dealing with pervasive low expectations. Sonia called it *coraje* (anger), Belinda called it winning, and Benito called it inspiration.

Sonia's positive nature helped her overcome negative challenges even in a state of anger. "Well, if you told me that I can't do it or you told me that no, I'll never make it, I fill up with *coraje* [anger]. Well, I'll show you I can make it. And I will" (SR, 305–308). Sonia was very competitive and more persistent when people tried to discourage her.

Belinda had the same determination when she was not expected to compete. She did whatever it took to get it done. "Sir, I'm going to win the district championship. I don't care how long we have to practice. I don't care what we have to do sir, I want to win" (RG, 240–243). In elementary school, she felt her competence was questioned when she was placed in the less challenging classes "because that's what our teacher would tell us. Even our own teacher would tell us they were the smart class. I wanted to be in the other class with the smart students, the ones who spoke English" (BM, 121–125). All Belinda really wanted was an opportunity to prove herself and she never stopped trying to get this chance even through high school.

> I wanted to be in that GT class. The counselor did not let me change because he said I didn't have good achievement test scores. . . .I kept telling him that I could do G.T. work and I would show him if he just gave me a chance. He refused to change me because of my scores. (BM, 427–437)

Benito approached these difficult situations using the same approach. Not all people knew his potential. "I remember going to the counselor and telling her I wanted to go to college and she told me that I should consider a vocational school and that sort of thing." He remembers a teacher that almost convinced him he was not capable when he did not allow him to take Algebra. "Mr. Pérez said I was just an average student and I was not allowed to register because I didn't have the scores. I began to think that maybe he was right and that I was just an average student" (BG, 201–203). Benito was inspired when people tried to persuade him that he was incapable.

> When people tell me, you don't have the money or *¿como le vas a hacer?* [how are you going to do it]? Those things tend to inspire some people and I'm one of those people that *me pongo más terco* [I get more stubborn]. I'm going to show them because I don't like to lose. (BG, 350–357)

Sonia, Belinda and Benito have been relentless in their struggle to live their dreams. Their ability to overcome adversity has been a lifelong learning process. At every stage of their lives they relied on their personal resources to maintain a high level of confidence and self-esteem.

LESSONS LEARNED ABOUT CRITICAL ETHNOGRAPHY AND PEDAGOGY

✣

Because we're wetbacks the law is always after us,
Because we're illegal and don't speak English
The gringo is determined to get us out, and we are determined
    to come back.
If some are kicked out through Laredo, they make it through
    Mexicali all right.
  If others are kicked out through Tijuana, six more come in
    through Nogales.
Just figure out how many enter each month.

(From Vivan los Mojados *by Luis Armnenta)*

The exploitation of cheap labor has serious long-term effects. "Today's official 'guest workers' (a dubious claim that cannot be considered here), become tomorrow's 'ghost workers'" (Suárez-Orozco, 1998b, p. 301). The efforts by California politicians on behalf of big business seem to have produced the largest wave of undocumented workers in the history of the state. As noted by Suárez-Orozco, "The ghost workers must at once 'be there' (to do the impossible jobs) but not be there (be voiceless and transparent)" (1998b, p. 301). With the ghost workers come the ghost industries that protect all the dirty little secrets of employers who abuse undocumented workers but cannot be prosecuted because they protect themselves by accepting false documents as proof of legitimate right to enter the country and seek employment. The *bracero* program offers a strong symbolic sense:

> *Bracero* comes from the Spanish word *brazos* meaning "arms": the arms needed to do the work. But instead of "arms" whole human beings came to do these jobs. The tension here is between two meaning systems: a system that constructs these workers as invisible ghosts or disembodied "arms" and a system that insists on their humanity. The discursive movement from guest workers as "arms" to guest workers as human beings, with needs, with families, with children in need of basic services such as schooling—in short workers qua humanity—is what is most subversive to the regime. (Suárez-Orozco, 1998b, p. 301)

This Ethnographic Research Project

The topic for this study has arisen from our personal interest and passion for the well-being of all children and our commitment to creating space for those children who follow. As teachers, teacher trainers, counselors, principals, and professors, we have worked with many culturally different children such as Sonia, Belinda, and Benito. We have lived the same kind of experiences as these children. We are rich with experiences that help us see the world and understand society in ways that permit us to understand better the success, failure, and pain of immigrant, migrant children. We understand the power we have as teachers, counselors, or administrators over the lives of the students we serve.

The review of the literature about Mexican and Hispanic migrant students was not very encouraging. The searches we conducted produced literature that focused mostly on the failure of immigrant, migrant farm worker students. Mobility is the major factor impacting their lives as students. Most migrant students attend two to three schools within a year and are usually overage in grade level by 1–2 years. The average level of education for the head of a migrant family was 6 years in 1986 (Harrington, 1987). This special population has the highest school failure and dropout rates (Straits, 1987). They have the lowest graduation rate of any population group in the public schools. Migrant educators place the dropout rate for migrant students anywhere from 50–90% (Interstate Migrant Education Council, 1987). The Migrant Attrition Project conducted a study that showed a 45% national dropout rate, whereas a study done 12 years earlier had reported a 90% dropout rate (Salerno, 1991). Not much has changed for this group of students in U.S. schools or in the fields.

Given the pervasive nature of these studies, it is not surprising why teachers have developed such low expectations of these students. This type of literature has failed to generate effective long-term solutions. Migrant students have been placed in demeaning and stigmatizing remedial pullout programs that have served to perpetuate negative teacher attitudes and low expectations about Mexican students in general. These findings validated the apparent need for this study. Our goal is to portray these students as capable and competent in spite of their "cultural disadvantages." The main purpose of this study was to elucidate the resiliency and the amazingly successful life journeys of these migrant students who seem academically invulnerable. We hope these stories will incite the readers, practitioners, and policymakers to transition from the primary phase of awareness to the more advanced phase of pedagogical innovation. Most importantly, however, it is our hope that this study will change attitudes and raises expectations about the capabilities and competence of Mexican migrant students.

The study uses a qualitative approach (especially critical ethnography) to examine in depth the lives of three migrant students and their families. Because there are not many studies that have focused on success stories of Mexican migrant students, the participants chosen for this study were all successful in school. They were selected using purposive intensity sampling. This type of sampling facilitated the selection of information-rich cases for study that displayed the particular phenomenon of interest of the researcher (Patton, 1990). They were purposively selected to represent the following criteria: they must have been migrant farm workers and successful students, based on their grades and ability to graduate from high school. They were also representative of different groups in terms of age, educational experience, and gender. Two were female and one was male. One particular participant (female) was a high school senior (now at St. Edward's University), one (female) was a senior in college (now a graduate from St. Edward's University), and the oldest (male) was a college graduate (now a lawyer).

We collected data through in-depth ethnographic interviews, observations, and review of documents and records. The in-depth, open-ended interview was the main source of data collection. We conducted numerous interviews with the participants and several with their families and significant others. The open-ended questions were designed to elicit detailed descriptions of the lives of the participants. Extensive field notes from a long series of observations were also a significant source of data. The advantage of direct observation "is that it provides here-and-now experience in depth" (Guba & Lincoln, 1985, p. 273). A detailed field note journal of these observations was compiled for continuous review and analysis. Another important source of data were school records and documents such as academic records, report cards, and transcripts.

Audiotapes were transcribed following each interview and preliminary interpretation of the results was conducted. Each interview analysis generated additional questions for clarification and inquiry. Cross validation was performed through the data collected from interviews with parents, teachers, and others. Member checks were conducted with each of the participants following the first draft of each case study. Each participant was provided a copy to review. They responded with clarifications, corrections, and additional information.

We have interpreted the interview data using theoretical and narrative or descriptive analytic strategies. Data interpretation started during single interviews, and proceeded from interview to interview and from observation to observation. Initially, a case-by-case analysis was done employing the narrative/descriptive approach. As each case analysis was completed, cross-case analysis was conducted using theoretical propositions to begin the process of grouping together data from different participants and to generate categories, themes, and patterns (Guba & Lincoln, 1985).

It is important to note that the participants and the authors have similar backgrounds and life experiences. Without a doubt, this similarity has influenced our interpretation in one way or another. Whereas it may have biased our perspective, it also served as a tool to see beyond what was not said or directly observed. As participants shared their lives with us, we relived our own. We could sense what they were feeling, and identified with what they were thinking. Heuristics brings to the fore the personal experience and insights of the researcher. Heuristic inquiry focuses on intense human experiences, intense from the point of view of the investigator....It is a combination of personal experience and intensity that yield an understanding of the essence of the phenomenon. (Patton, 1990, p. 71)

The salient effect of heuristics is the relationship that develops between the researcher and the participants to clarify the nature and meaning of their experiences. We grew closer to the participants as our relationships evolved. We were aware that our ways of knowing and interpretation was susceptible to prejudices, and we realized quickly that making assumptions or generalizations before looking at all the data could be problematic. We learned this from the beginning with the family of the first participant.

What is at stake when we succeed? Successful children assimilate at the risk of losing what helped them break the cycle in the first place. It is almost like losing by succeeding. The system is justified because we become part of it. It is overwhelming we either succeed or fall into the trap of helping to perpetuate it, or we fail and it succeeds by locking us in the subordinate roles assigned to us by the hegemonic culture. In this sense, as Foley (1990) suggested, schools are indeed systems of social reproduction.

Our original intent with this study was to report the amazing life stories of three academically invulnerable migrant students. In the process, we developed close relationships with the participants and their parents. We learned many things about them, and they learned many things about us. This experience has taught us much more than we ever imagined. The stories we shared with each other provided opportunities for reflection. Benito expressed,

> I've never really sat down and sort of looked back to think. Participating in the study has forced me to look backwards. It's the first time that I've actually done some reflective kinds of things and tried to verbalize it. (BM)

In facilitating this process, we also had the opportunity to contemplate our own lives. The most powerful revelation we experienced was that for a long time we had been trying to break away from what made us who we are. We got caught up in the race to success without knowing there was no finish line. We intentionally tried to bring up our own sons and daughters differently, and we were determined that they would not "suffer" the way we had. We came to realize that growing up we had not "suffered" to the degree we previously believed. For a long time we felt we were also *pobrecitos,* yet we did not want our children to ever be *pobrecitos* themselves. Upon reflection, we are not so sure that our sons and daughters are as socially prepared to go out into the real world as we were at their age. Therefore, the ideal would be to negotiate through the system without discarding or forgetting identity and roots. It is ironic that a lifestyle that deemed us "culturally disadvantaged" and bestowed upon us the low expectations of a deficit-thinking society is also the lifestyle that empowered us to become resilient and invulnerable.

Lessons Learned from the Study

One of the most important lessons learned from working with immigrant, migrant populations is to realize how little we know about them, how unprepared we are to study their school achievement and adaptation to American society, and how ethnocentric researchers and instructional personnel can be handling cultural and linguistic differences in children. A number of healthy new approaches have become extremely popular: sociolinguistic analysis, ethnographic methods, critical pedagogy, and comparative approaches. This volume illustrates some of these approaches. The case studies all form part of a critical approach to discovering cultural differences, achievement motivation, and resiliency. Perhaps a generic term to encompass some of these approaches is critical ethnography. The central question is how we can learn from critical ethnography to generate more creative and effective instructional approaches.

How can critical ethnography help document the educational needs, assets, and problems of Mexican migrant children, as well as their unexpected successes? How can teachers move from ethnographic accounts to a constructive pedagogy that can lead children to lasting empowerment via educational achievement? Indeed, to understand better the relationship between ethnographic research and pedagogical praxis, it is essential to examine the fundamental character of empowerment from a pedagogical standpoint as the successful acquisition of higher level cognitive skills that permit children to learn effectively in school. A pedagogy of hope is only possible if educators can go beyond the rhetoric of critical discourse to a deeper understanding of intellectual development (Vigotsky, 1962, 1978) as the means to break the cycle of underachievement and oppression, away from hegemonic instructional structures.

A number of ethnographers have dealt with problems of adaptation of immigrant children in the context of the school environment (Bartolomé & Macedo, 1997; Delgado-Gaitan, 1994; Delgado-Gaitan & Trueba,

1991; Deyle & Margonis, 1995; Gutierrez, 1994; Gutierrez, Larson, & Kreuter, 1995; Patthey-Chavez, 1993; Trueba, 1987, 1997; Trueba, Cheng, & Ima, 1993; Trueba et al., 1990; Trueba, Rodriguez et al., 1993; Trueba & Zou, 1994, 1998; Wilson, 1991). Often these scholars have used critical theory in an effort to design "transformative" strategies for teachers and students (based on Freire, 1973, 1995; scholars such as Freire & Macedo, 1987, 1996; Giroux & McLaren 1994; McLaren, 1995, 1997). The efforts, however, have not clarified the transition from an ethnographic or ethno-historical account of oppression to a pedagogy of hope. This transition must take into account the instructional context and children's need to acquire critical thinking skills to prepare them to be fully in control of their lives without forcing them to lose their ethnic and cultural identities. Some of the accounts of liberation in a culturally congruent way are genuinely Vygotskian in nature and open the door to a "Vigotskian pedagogy of hope" anchored in the research process.

As Suárez-Orozco (1998b) has pointed out, the United States is experiencing national hardship. Widespread job insecurity abounds alongside of an increase in crime, and a crisis in family values. These anxieties have targeted immigrants and refugees as the source of the problems in American society and the cause of our deep and "terrifying sense of homelessness". To compound these anti-immigrant feelings, it seems as if Latino immigrants arrive with a lower educational level and are unable to achieve academically as well as mainstream children. A number of scholars have stated that the education of Latinos is worse off now than in the previous decade (Portes, 1996; Suárez-Orozco & Suárez-Orozco, 1995a, 1995b; Valencia, 1991). Yet, some studies documenting relative academic success of Mexican immigrants in high school have invited reflection on the supportive role of the family and home environment (Díaz Salcedo, 1996). The narratives collected in this volume and elsewhere (Trueba, 1997) about academic achievement, in the midst of the narratives of inequity for Mexican immigrant students, represent success where many expected failure.

The fact that so many of these children succeed in schools may be linked to factors that enhance their successful binational adaptation. The role of women in the maintenance of the Spanish language and Mexican culture seems to have played a key role in the long-term adaptation of Mexican immigrant families (Hondagneu-Sotelo, 1994; Trueba, 1997). Many factors contribute to the retention of the Spanish language—the critical mass of immigrants who speak the language, the frequent visits to hometowns and cities, and the interdependence between the families living on both sides of the border. The organization of functional networks of these families and their friends has been most instrumental in the survival of families during difficult economic times, but it has also served as very strong emotional support system to retain a cogent Mexican identity in the face of the traumas alluded to above by Suárez-Oroscos (1995a, 1995b; also Suárez-Orosco 1998). The substantial, although informal, financial cooperative system can also become a powerful political base from which to demand respect for their educational rights, as was the case in central California (Trueba, 1997). Organizations that had a religious character in the Mexican tradition became a vital political enclave and support system in their adaptation to this country (Trueba, Rodriguez et al., 1993). The only way for these families to engage in long-term economic ventures (buying land in Mexico, purchasing homes in the United States, and so on) is through the collective security of the family networks on both sides of the border, their collective savings, and their commitment to assist one another in times of crisis. The skill to survive emotionally and economically in the worst of situations continues to be a unique characteristic of many immigrant families who strategically invest every possible resource they may find. These resources are often obtained through their binational networks.

This "know-how" that Freire (1973, p. 10) called "knowing the world," in contrast with literacy as "knowing the word," is often the key factor in the survival and adaptation of the immigrant family on both sides of the border. We immigrants and children of immigrants are now the ethnographers and must face the difficult task of coming to terms with our own identity crisis, as well as with conducting serious, scientific, and credible research. We have to deal with conflicts between our personal loyalties as members of ethnic communities and members of an elite group of social scientists. Sofía Villenas (1996) has described these conflicts and dilemmas as follows:

> Geographically, politically, and economically, I have lived under the same yoke of colonization as the Chicano communities I study, experiencing the same discrimination and alienation from mainstream society that comes from being a member of a caste "minority."…Racially and ethnically I am *indígena*, a detribalized Native American woman,

descendant of the Quechua-speaking people of the South American Andes. Politically I am a Chicana, born and raised in the American Southwest, in the legendary territories of Aztlán. (p. 712)

Villenas concluded with a remarkable insight,

> We the new generation of "native" ethnographers, including myself, increasingly working within and writing about our own communities, we are beginning to question how our histories and identities are entangled in the workings of domination and we engage the oppressive discourses of "othering." (p. 729).

Critical ethnographic practice demands a conscious realization of the risks and epistemological challenges researchers must face.

Critical Ethnography

A modern concept of critical ethnography as a research methodology stresses the notion that *all* education is intrinsically political, and consequently critical ethnography must advocate for the oppressed by

1. Documenting the nature of oppression
2. Documenting the process of empowerment—a journey away from oppression
3. Accelerating the conscientization of the oppressed and the oppressors—without this reflective awareness of the rights and obligations of humans there is no way to conceptualize empowerment, equity, and a struggle of liberation
4. Sensitizing the research community to the implications of research for the quality of life—clearly linking intellectual work to real-life conditions and
5. Reaching a higher level of understanding of the historical, political, sociological, and economic factors supporting the abuse of power and oppression, of neglect and disregard for human rights, and of the mechanisms to learn and internalize rights and obligations.

Ultimately what the above means is that there is an intimate relationship between the intellectual activity of research and the praxis of the daily life of researchers. Praxis (in Freire's sense of political commitment to struggle for liberation and in defense of human rights) is the ultimate goal of critical ethnography. This praxis must encompass a global and cross-cultural commitment to advocate for the rights of all humankind and, thus, to create human solidarity against oppression (Freire, 1973, 1995). Critical ethnography has deep theoretical roots in psychological anthropology and was later refined in sociology and philosophy by the seminal work of Paulo Freire. The goal of early anthropologists was to improve the schooling and overall human development of all children, as revealed in a conference held at Stanford University on June 9–14, 1954, organized by George Spindler. Renowned scholars such as Solon T. Kimball, Alfred L. Kroeber, Dorothy Lee, Margaret Mead, Felix M. Keesing, John Gillin, and Cora DuBois shared their concerns relating to the overall development of all children, the preparation of ethnically diverse children, and the need to pursue pedagogically appropriate methods of teaching (Spindler, 1995).

Why is critical ethnography a significant methodological tool, and what is its relationship to Vygotskian theories of cognitive development and adequate pedagogies as applied to the Mexican immigrant children? What are children's basic developmental and academic needs? It is not enough to recognize the presence of oppression and to criticize schooling, teachers, and social systems. The task is to do all those things and move towards a realistic pedagogy that links the creation of viable pedagogies to children's empowerment.

For most critical theorists, oppression is not only the result of class struggle but also the result of structural elements perpetuated through cultural patterns leading to the perpetuation of economic, political, and other semiotic systems that violate human rights, especially the right to learn. Culture comes into the picture, not only from the standpoint of the oppressor's lifestyle, values, and the assumptions of superiority over others, but also as a socially structured set of relationships, expectations, and accepted practices. Culture must be redefined in a way that illuminates the relationship between oppression and the lifestyle of the oppressor, between universal rights for all, and the unique rights of the few justified on the basis of cultural traditions. Culture, therefore, is not just what people do, what they believe, and how they act, but also the consequences of how people live and act for the less privileged. In the early 1960s the classical definitions of culture included a complex set of values, traditions, lifestyles, and behavior patterns characterizing particular human groups and distinguishing them from one another; furthermore, culture was observable and transmitted from one generation to another. In the late 1960s and early 1970s culture became an integral part of the *cognitive revolution* that explored various conceptual configurations.

The historical changes in the concept of culture, from something out there to observe to something in people's heads, or cognitive configurations, affected anthropology, linguistics, and psychology (Shweder, 1996). The cognitive revolution moved the emphasis from observed behavior outside of the actors to the study of language as a window to understand cognitive structures inside of the actors. In other words, what Shweder called "mental-state language" dealing with beliefs, desires, plans, wants, emotions, goals, feelings, which revealed a code and set of values that permitted ethnographers to make inferences. Ethnographers had to use mental-state language as accessible and public experiences (rather than inaccessible and private experiences) subject to external and inter subjective interpretation. There are serious challenges involved in doing critical ethnographic research because the process itself is not altogether clear. It is a means of inquiry as well as a means of transformation. Some view it as inherently "colonizing" and "exploitative." In some sense, all social science research is suspected of being hegemonic, colonizing, and even objectifying people while it attempts to understand them. "This contradiction (between ethnography's 'exemplary status' and its 'colonial nature') instantiates the more generalized social division of intellectual and manual labor . . . [whereby] research is posited only as the professional activity of the privileged minority" (DeGenova, 1997, p. 1).

McLaren and da Silva (1993) remarked that "emancipatory knowledge is never realized fully, but is continually dreamed, continually revived, and continually transformed in the heart of our memories, the flames of our longing and the passion of our struggle" (p. 59). Critical ethnography permits researchers to get into the emancipatory knowledge that motivates ethnic minority students' resistance to the dominant culture in America. However, critical ethnography remains at the level of detached discourse, without describing how to take the emancipation route and to construct an effective pedagogy. Critical ethnography, as a tool to reflect seriously on equity matters from inside perspectives (from the perspective of the oppressed), is intended to facilitate the examination of cultural hegemonic practices and to document cultural conflict as a drama taking place in the classroom. This is done via reflection on historical factors of ethnic and racial legitimacy, reproduction of the social order, and the right to a voice in one's own language (Leistyna, Woodrum, & Sherblom, 1996). Critical ethnography used to document inequity is a risky and painful type of research, the kind that, at times, ethnographers find frustrating and sterile, narcissistic and selfish, insightful but deprived of social consequences for real life. It often leads researchers to the conviction that they "do not want to know too many of the details. They want to explain social inequality by blaming the victims or in any other way that leaves their accustomed identities intact. They are afraid of being wounded" (Carspecken, 1996, pp. 170–171).

A Vygotskian Pedagogy of Hope

Because critical ethnography as a research tool entails a commitment to praxis, discourse alone is insufficient and even offensive in the absence of emancipatory action, of praxis. Research with Mexican migrant immigrants was no exception, and the praxis associated with our inquiries about their resilience and their relative success in surviving culturally and psychologically did not take away our pain. We wanted to understand how relatively powerless Mexican immigrant people created a system of resistance to dominant beliefs, values, norms, and practices, and why this resistance can frighten some other persons. But also we wanted to understand how school children, assisted by their teachers and parents (especially their mothers), construct for themselves a genuine Utopia for a better future, and dream about becoming engineers, architects, business persons, or technicians. For example, in the case of our participants, when middle and high school Mexican students saw their parents come home full of mud, smelly after working all day in the fields, burned by the sun and the wind, hungry and in pain with premature arthritis and a face of exhaustion, their commitment to pursue their dreams became stronger.

Mexican immigrant women who defend their cultural integrity in all arenas, especially in the schools, can appear even more frightening. A pedagogy of hope based on Vygotskian principles establishes the relationship between culture, language, and cognition as the foundation to acquire knowledge. The role of culture in mediating the transmission of knowledge and intellectual growth is crucial. The mediation through appropriate cultural symbols in the construction of academic knowledge (or via "assisted performance") must translate instruction into pedagogical practices that permit immigrant children to engage in their own development, to invest their own cultural and linguistic capital, and to advance without prejudice. The research in schools conducted by Kris Gutiérrez and her colleagues (Gutiérrez, 1994; Gutiérrez, Larson, & Kreuter, 1995; Gutiérrez, Rymes, & Larson, 1995) is a clear example of critical ethnography with an understanding of the developmental principles that Vygotsky and neo-Vygotskians have established. This research not only disclosed hegemonic structures of teachers, but also opened new interactional and curricular strategies to capitalize on the linguistic and cultural richness of children's background through an intensive collaborative, joint construction of knowledge in the classroom.

In spite of the inherent challenges and difficulties faced by ethnographers, critical ethnography with a Vygotskian perspective continues to be one of the most promising fields. In the hands of educational researchers committed to sound pedagogy and the full development of immigrant children, it is a new avenue to create a pedagogy of hope in actual instruction. This type of critical ethnography is based on the principles of assisted performance within the zone of proximal development established by Vygotsky (1962, 1978) and practiced today by neo-Vygotskians (Cole, 1990, 1997; Moll, 1990; Trueba 1991; Wertsch, 1981, 1985, 1991). The combination of the principles of critical ethnography (consistent with Paulo Freire's pedagogy of hope) is compatible with, and complementary to, the principles of the sociohistorical school of psychology represented by the work of Vygotsky and neo-Vygotskians.

One of the most important contributions of Vygotsky to understanding of immigrant children's intellectual development and school achievement, especially those undergoing rapid sociocultural change, was his theory about the relationship between cognitive and social phenomena. Vygotsky stated that the development of uniquely human higher level mental functions such as consciousness and the creation of taxonomic cognitive structures (required for academic learning) find their origin in day-to-day social interaction. Vygotsky searched in daily social lives for the origins of human consciousness and higher level mental functions.

According to Moll (1990), if teachers follow Vygotskian principles, they will see literacy as "the understanding and communication of meaning" and will make efforts "to make classrooms literate environments in which many language experiences can take place and different types of literacies can be developed and learned" (p. 8). Indeed, Moll stressed the following idea:

Teachers who follow this approach reject rote instruction or reducing reading and writing into skill sequences taught in isolation or a successive, stage-like manner. Rather, they emphasize the creation of social contexts in which children actively learn to use, try, and manipulate language in the service of making sense or creating meaning. (p. 8)

Effective teachers who understand the process of internalization that permits students to make the transition from interpsychological experience to intrapsychological cognitive categories adopt culturally and linguistically meaningful teaching strategies (Vygotsky, 1962, 1978), that is, strategies occurring within the zone of proximal development of children. The *zone of proximal development* was defined by Vygotsky (1978) as the distance between a child's "actual developmental level as determined by independent problem-solving" and the higher level of "potential development as determined through problem solving under adult guidance or in collaboration with more capable peers" (p. 86). Furthermore, the intimate relationship between language and thought proposed by Vygotsky (language as a symbolic system mediating all social and cognitive functions) implies a link between the lower intellectual development and school achievement of some immigrant children and the abrupt transition from a familiar to an unfamiliar sociocultural environment, and therefore, to the lack of both linguistic and cultural knowledge to interact meaningfully with adults and peers. Consequently, no suitable zones of proximal development are opened up for them by adults or more informed peers, and the discourse and cognitive categories required to function in school are not readily available to them (Brown, Campione, Cole, Griffin, Mehan, & Riel, 1982; Trueba, 1991).

It is impossible to create appropriate zones of proximal development in oppressive and unfamiliar learning environments without the symbolic tools that allow a child to make sense of social transactions and to translate them into intrapsychological phenomena. However, a bilingual and bicultural teacher who understands the predicament of immigrant children can expand the zone of proximal development by creating a culturally familiar environment and establishing a personal relationship with immigrant students. The use of these zones of proximal development requires not only awareness of the relationship between language, thought, and culture, but also the appropriate pedagogical principles. A Vygotskian pedagogy requires that children become active engineers of their own learning and play a key role in determining the next intellectual challenge in their development. This pedagogy does not occur in a classroom where hegemonic discourse silences culturally and linguistically diverse children.

In a profoundly genuine sense, social and intellectual life is assisted performance in one way or another, especially for children as they become acquainted with complex symbolic systems that form constellations of cognitive domains. If the basic Vygotskian tenet is kept in mind, that is, that children's intellectual development is measured by their ability to solve problems "unassisted," then effective teaching must prepare them to solve problems on their own. For this, it is important to identify the complex social systems surrounding children and consequently their ability to manipulate such systems. Special assistance (effective teaching) is needed by children who are in transition from one cultural and linguistic system to another. Immigrant children by definition are in transition, and they feel particularly vulnerable in instructional settings that presuppose knowledge of symbolic and cognitive systems familiar only to local children who belong to a given culture and society. Effective teaching must take into consideration the unique zone of proximal development (ZPD) of culturally and linguistically different children.

Tharp and Gallimore (1988) defined teaching as follows:

> Distinguishing *the proximal zone* from the *developmental level* by contrasting assisted versus unassisted performance has profound implications for educational practice. It is in the proximal zone that teaching may be defined in terms of child development. In Vygotskian terms, teaching is good only when it *"awakens and rouses to life those functions which are in a stage of maturing, which lie in the zone of proximal development."*... We can therefore derive this general definition of teaching: *Teaching consists in assisting performance through the ZPD. Teaching can be said to occur when assistance is offered at points in the ZPD at which performance requires assistance* (p. 31; italics in original).

There are many ways to assist children, to teach children within their zone of proximal development. A precondition, however, to teach them effectively is to establish a trusting relationship that permits an adult to model for the child, to engage in contingency managing, providing feedback, guiding, questioning and organizing structurally cognitive domains. These important types of assistance must be calibrated to the children in ways that open up new avenues for intellectual growth. For a teacher to do this in a regular classroom is difficult enough; he or she must be able to "read" the children and feel their grasp of ideas and their level of comprehension. But with children in transition, whose bilingual skills vary a great deal, a teacher must be prepared to be especially flexible.

The ability to learn among immigrant children is also contingent upon a minimum of continuity between the home learning environment and the school environment. Children must acquire a basic ability to understand their personal lives and their family's struggle to defend their rights in a larger society. They must understand the vicarious experience of oppression and must conceptualize education as the way out of oppression for themselves and their parents.

How did the children in this study handle the racism and verbal abuses from peers and even teachers? Their response was: "As our parents have taught us, we'll show them with our grades that we can succeed." The intimate relationship between the knowledge of the word (academic achievement) and the knowledge of the world (the politics of success in school) gave Mexican immigrant children and youth the basis for survival, for resilience. This is consistent with Vygotsky's theory of development (Cole, 1997; Vygotsky, 1962, 1978; Wertsch, 1981, 1985, 1991) and Freire's broad concept of literacy (Freire, 1973, 1995; Freire & Macedo, 1987, 1996).

Concluding Thoughts

Why did Sonia, Belinda, and Benito become psychologically resilient and academically invulnerable? According to Benard (1991), an academically invulnerable and resilient child is one who has

1. The ability to establish and keep meaningful relationships with others,
2. Developed problem-solving skills that enhance his/her ability to make wise choices,

3. A strong sense of autonomy, and
4. A strong sense of purpose and future.

They succeeded because they were able to develop extraordinary protective resources. Their personal and environmental resources perpetuated each other. As young children, their parents provided the essential security that protected them while they formed support within their schools. As their support system evolved, their personal resources were enhanced. By the same token, as their pool of personal resources grew, their ability to form meaningful relationships increased accordingly. The level of interaction between sociocultural, personal, and environmental factors determined the degree of invulnerability and success. This helped to mediate the mitigating effects of stressful life events that resulted from challenging sociocultural factors.

We grew up in families that taught us respect and pride and gave us a sense of hope. Our parents modeled a strong work ethic as we watched them working in the fields without complaining, day in and day out. Though resources were limited, there was always enough for all of us. We worked together in the fields for one common cause and purpose. We could make concrete connections between hard work and the food on our tables. We knew where our food, clothing, and shelter came from. Though we were poor, there was always a sense of pride. We learned to respect others but especially ourselves. This sense of pride helped us cope with the pain of cruelty when others made fun of the way we dressed, our language, and our family.

Our parents valued education highly. They encouraged us to break away from their way of living without making us feel ashamed. Our parents were proud of who they were, but they had high expectations for all their children. There was never a doubt that we were expected to graduate from high school and go to college. A strong sense of family support kept us from falling through the cracks while we established a support system within the schools. This gave us time to learn the rules of the game we were expected to play. In the process we found caring teachers that encouraged us to break the cycle of migrancy without making us feel inferior about our way of living. They dignified our lifestyle while we were living it and raised our sense of self-worth.

When children from culturally different backgrounds enroll in schools, they come with certain qualities, personalities, and behavioral characteristics. These are often viewed as vulnerabilities or risk factors. Depending on the way the schools react to these characteristics, they are seen as either risk factors or protective resources. Some children's characteristics are congruent with the demands of schools, but many others come with behavioral attributes that are not compatible with school norms. Their skills and experiences may be different, but they are not developmentally delayed, low ability, or less capable (Kagan, 1991; Meisels, Dorfman, & Steele, 1992). Negotiating the transition from home to school successfully depends on the ability to master some critical social behaviors that are related to school. Therefore, it is the responsibility of the schools to facilitate this process. It is the obligation of the teachers to help students maintain their feelings of self-worth while they develop the personal resources to play by the new rules. Teachers can help make this a smooth and seamless transition from home to school without stripping their students of dignity.

Facilitating success for all students is not a complicated process. All it takes is an individual philosophy of genuine caring that must be systemically pervasive across the organization of the school. At the micro level, it takes teachers who look at diversity as an advantage rather than a disadvantage. Diversity in schools is not a new phenomenon. Students have always had socioeconomic, cultural, and linguistic differences. The significant difference today is the hyper-awareness that all students deserve and must be provided with equal and equitable opportunities to an education free of stigmatizing labels. It is the duty of teachers to embrace diversity and to honor the characteristic differences of all students. Teachers must adapt to and dignify the value system the children bring from home. They must find ways to empower their students as they help them find and use the inherent strengths of their lifestyle. Caring teachers are able to see the possibilities in each child.

At the macro level, it takes a group of caring teachers and a principal or leader with high expectations to provide a school-wide climate of caring and support for every child. Children are always treated with dignity and respect. When students feel valued and cared for in school, they are more apt to be motivated intrinsically to please the people they love and trust. Academic success is achieved more naturally when schools focus on what really matters in life for students (Noddings, 1988, 1992). Programs must be designed to draw from the unique strengths of the children rather than categorizing children into special programs based on their unique needs (deficits). Schools must build on and use the knowledge, experiences, skills, and language that children bring to school. Teachers need to connect and apply children's prior cultural knowledge to learning the values, skills, language, and knowledge expected at school. Schools must seek ways to foster the protective resources children have learned at home. However, this would require more than just believing and expecting that each student have knowledge and experience to contribute to the teaching and learning process. Students must also be facilitated with opportunities to demonstrate their strengths and knowledge. Furthermore, they need to feel that their strengths and knowledge are acknowledged and valued.

APPENDIX

⌁

Belinda

One of the authors has known Belinda Magallán since she was a seventh grader in Rio Grande City, Texas. He was her middle school counselor. As we began to plan this study, Belinda was one of several migrant students that came to our minds. She met all the criteria, and we knew she would be an excellent representative for the study. We had the opportunity to work with Belinda, and got to know her very well.

As a counselor, one of the authors dealt with many migrant students. Belinda was one of these students. She was an average student waiting to be discovered. Teachers did not know much about her except that she was a migrant. She was lost within the larger group as she fought the system for a chance to prove herself. Today, Belinda is in transition. She is a college graduate seeking employment to begin her professional career.

Benito

Benito García is the oldest of the three participants in this study. He is representative of those that have made it through the public school system, college, and have become professionally successful.

When we began thinking of candidates for this study, Benito's name had been mentioned as a possible participant by several of our nomination sources. In addition, one of the authors had known Benito since he was very young because they are from the same hometown. He first knew him through his youngest brother. They went to school together from Head Start through college graduation at Sul Ross State University.

Benito met all the selection criteria; we knew he had lived in poverty, and we also knew about his success as an adult. What we did not know, however, was how extraordinary his adventure through life had been. This amazing excursion began before he was born when his mother decided to come to this country from México.

Sonia

Washington is the fourth largest receiving state for migrant farm workers and students from Texas (MSRTS, 1994). Most of these students come from the Rio Grande Valley. In the summer of 1993, one of the authors worked in Washington at the Mt. Vernon migrant summer evening program. He worked with many migrant students like Sonia that summer. He met many academically successful migrant students who were attending the summer program. Thus, at the time of this study, it became evident that we should return to Washington to find a participant who would meet the study's criteria.

Prior to meeting Sonia, in the spring of 1996, one of the authors began to make plans for a trip to Washington to gather data and begin fieldwork. We called several acquaintances that work with migrant programs in Washington to assist in identifying a qualified participant. In the process, one of the authors was offered a job as director of a home-based summer program for migrant students in Prosser, Washington (eastern Washington). He accepted the job because it offered an opportunity to visit and work with migrant students and families in their homes.

Everything seemed to fall into place smoothly, but after two weeks of intense fieldwork, our study began to fall apart when the first participant's father decided not to let him continue. We were disappointed, frustrated, and desperate. Pressed for time, we had practically given up on finding another student in Washington.

Fortunately, we came across a young woman who met the criteria for participation. Through Cristóbal, Sonia's brother, we invited her to the summer evening program so we could talk to her. We interviewed her via telephone and asked her about her grades, graduation, classes, college plans, and other general information. We were convinced that she met the obvious criteria. We decided to make the trip from Sunnyside, Washington, to meet with her parents and get their approval for her participation. This is how and when our relationship with the Ramírez family began. We met Sonia Ramírez and her family in July of 1996 at the Sunset labor camp in the state of Washington. She was 17 years old when we first started to work with her.

REFERENCES

Alva, S. A., & Padilla, A. M. (1995). Academic invulnerability among Mexican Americans: A conceptual framework. *Journal of Educational Issues of Language Minority Students.* Available: www.ncbe.gwu.edu/miscpubs/jeilms/vol15/academic.html

Arias, M. B. (1986). The context of education for Hispanic students: An overview. *American Journal of Education, 95,* 26–57.

Ascher, C. (1991). Highly mobile students: Educational problems and possible solutions. New York: ERIC Clearinghouse on Urban Education. (ERIC Digest ED 351–426)

Barrington, B. L., & Hendricks, B. (1989). Differentiating characteristics of high school graduates, dropouts, and nongraduates. *Journal of Educational Research, 82*(6), 309–319.

Bartolomé, L. (1996). Beyond the methods fetish: Toward a humanizing pedagogy. In P. Leistyna, A. Woodrum, & S. Sherblom (Eds.), *Breaking free: The transformative power of critical pedagogy* (Harvard Education Review, Reprint Series no. 27, pp. 229–252). Cambridge, MA: Harvard Educational Review.

Bartolomé, L., & Macedo, D. (1997). Dancing with bigotry: The poisoning of racial and cultural identities. *Harvard Educational Review, 67*(2), 222–242.

Benard, B. (1991). *Fostering resiliency in kids: Protective factors in the family, school, and community.* Portland, OR: Northwest Regional Educational Laboratory.

Benard, B. (1995). Fostering resiliency in urban schools. In B. Williams (Ed.), *Closing the achievement gap: A vision to guide change in beliefs and practice.* Oak Brook, IL: Research for Better Schools and North Central Regional Educational Laboratory.

Braddock, J. H. (1990). *Tracking: Implications for student race ethnic groups* (Report No. 1). Baltimore, MD: Johns Hopkins University, Center for Research on Effective Schooling for Disadvantaged Students.

Brown, A., Campione, E., Cole, M., Griffin, P., Mehan, H., & Riel, M. (1982). A models system for the study of learning difficulties. *The Quarterly Newsletter of the Laboratory of Comparative Human Cognition, 4*(3), 39–55.

References

Brown, G. H., Rosen, N. L., Hill, S. T., & Olivas, M. A. (1980). *The condition of education for Hispanic Americans* (NCES 80–303). Washington, DC: U.S. Government Printing Office.

Cárdenas, J. A., & Cárdenas, B. (1977). *The theory of incompatibilities.* San Antonio, TX: Intercultural Development Research Association.

Carspecken, P. F. (1996). *Critical ethnography in educational research: A theoretical and practical guide.* New York: Routledge.

Carter, T. P., & Segura, R. D. (1979). *Mexican Americans in school: A decade of change.* New York: College Entrance Examination Board.

Chavkin, N. F. (1991). *Family lives and parental involvement in migrant students' education.* Charleston, WV: ERIC Clearinghouse on Rural Education and Small Schools. (ERIC Digest ED 335 174)

Clark, R. M. (1983). *Family life and school achievement: Why poor black children succeed or fail.* Chicago, IL: The University of Chicago Press.

Cochran, E. (Ed.). (1992). Into the mainstream: Guidelines for teaching language minority students. New York: Instructional Resource Center.

Cohen S., & Syme, S. L. (Eds.). (1985). *Social support and health.* New York: Academic Press.

Cole, M. (1990). Cognitive development and formal schooling: The evidence from cross-cultural research. In L. Moll (Ed.), *Vygotsky and education: Instructional implications and applications of sociohistorical psychology* (pp. 89–110). Cambridge, MA: Cambridge University Press.

Cole, M. (1997). *Cultural psychology: A once and future discipline.* Cambridge, MA: Harvard University Press.

Coles, R. (1971). *Migrants, sharecroppers, mountaineers* (vol. 2). Boston, MA: Little, Brown.

Comer, J. P. (1988). Educating poor minority children. *Scientific American, 259*(5), 42–48.

Cox, J. L., Burkheimer, G., Curtin, T. R., Rudes, B., Iachan, R., Strang, W., Carlson, E., Zarkin, G., & Dean, N. (1992). *Final report: Descriptive study of the Chapter 1 Migrant Education Program. Vol. 1: Study findings and conclusions.* Prepared under contract for the U.S. Department of Education by Research Triangle Institute, Research Triangle, NC. Washington, DC: U.S. Department of Education, Planning and Evaluation Service.

Cross, T. L. (1995). Understanding family resiliency from a relational world view. In H. I. McCubbin, E. A. Thompson, A. I. Thompson, & J. E. Fromer (Eds.), Resiliency in ethnic minority families. Vol. I: Native and immigrant American families (p. 153). Madison, WI: University of Wisconsin.

De Mers, D. (1988, November). Migrant programs meet unique challenges. *National Head Start Bulletin,* 2–3.

DeGenova, N. (1997). *The production of language and the language of oppression: Mexican labor and the politics of ESL in Chicago factories.* Presented at the University of California Spencer Foundation Winter Forum, February 14–15, 1997, Los Angeles.

Delgado-Gaitan, C. (1994). Russian refugee families: Accommodating aspirations through education. *Anthropology and Education Quarterly, 25*(2), 137–155.

Delgado-Gaitan, C., & Trueba, H. T. (1991). *Crossing cultural borders: Education for immigrant families in America.* London, England: Falmer Press.

Deyhle, D., & Margonis F. (1995). Navajo mothers and daughters: Schools, jobs, and the family. *Anthropology and Education Quarterly, 16*(2), 135–167.

Díaz Salcedo, S. (1996). *Successful Latino students at the high school level: A case study of ten students.* Analytic doctoral paper, Harvard University.

Dussel Peters, E. (2000). *Polarizing Mexico: The impact of liberalization strategy.* Boulder, CO: Lynne Rienner.

Dyson, D. S. (1983). Utilizing available resources at the local level. *Migrant Education Fact Sheet.* Las Cruces, NM: ERIC Clearinghouse on Rural Education and Small Schools. (ERIC Digest ED 286 702)

Effland, J., Hamm, S., & Oliveira, V. (1993). *Hired farm labor use on fruit, vegetable, and horticultural specialty farms.* Washington, DC: U.S. Department of Agriculture.

Elementary and Secondary Education School Act of 1965. (1965). 20 USC 8801.

Fine, M. A., & Schwebel, A. I. (1991). Resiliency in black children from single-parent families. In W.A. Rhodes & W.K. Brown (Eds.), *Why some children succeed despite the odds* (pp. 23–40). New York: Praeger.

Foley, D. (1990). *Learning capitalist culture: Deep in the heart of Tejas.* Philadelphia: University of Pennsylvania Press.

Freire, P. (1973). *Pedagogy of the oppressed.* New York: Seabury Press.

Freire, P. (1995). *Pedagogy of hope: Reliving pedagogy of the oppressed.* Translated by Robert R. Barr. New York: Continuum.

Freire, P., & Macedo, D. (1987). *Literacy: Reading the word and reading the world.* Critical Studies in Education series. Boston, MA: Bergin and Garvey.

Freire, P., & Macedo, D. (1996). A dialogue: Culture, language, and race. In P. Leistyna, A. Woodrum, & S. Sherblom (Eds.), *Breaking free: The transformative power of critical pedagogy* (Harvard Education Review, Reprint Series no. 27, pp. 199–228). Cambridge, MA: Harvard Education Review.

Gamio, Manuel. (1930/1971). *Mexican immigration to the United States: A study of human migration and adjustment.* Chicago, IL: University of Chicago Press. (Reprint, originally published 1930)

Garmezy, N. (1983). Stressors in childhood. In N. Garmezy & M. Rutter (Eds.), *Stress, coping and development in childhood* (pp. 43–84). New York: MacGraw Hill.

Garmezy, N. (1991). Resiliency and vulnerability to adverse developmental outcomes associated with poverty. *American Behavioral Scientist, 34*(4), 416–430.

Garmezy, N. & Rutter, M. (Eds.). (1983). *Stress, coping and development in childhood.* New York: MacGraw Hill.

Giroux, H., & McLaren, P. (1994). *Between borders: Pedagogy and the politics of cultural studies.* New York and London: Routledge.

González Baker, S., Bean, F. D., Escobar Latapí, A., & Weintraub, S. (1998). U.S. Immigration policies and trends: The growing importance of migration from Mexico. In M. M. Suárez-Orozco (Ed.), *Crossings: Mexican immigration in interdisciplinary perspectives* (pp. 53–74). Cambridge, MA: Harvard University, D. Rockefeller Center for Latin American Studies.

Gore, S. (1981). Stress-buffering functions of social support: An appraisal and clarification of research models. In B. S. Dohrenwend & B. P. Dohrenwend (Eds.), *Stressful life events and their contexts,* (pp. 202–222). New York: Wiley.

Guba, E. G., & Lincoln, Y. S. (1985). *Naturalistic inquiry.* Newbury Park, CA: Sage.

Gutierrez, K. (1994). How talk, context, and script shape contexts for learning: A cross-case comparison of journal sharing. *Linguistics and Education, 5,* 335–365.

Gutierrez, K., Larson, J., & Kreuter, B. (1995). Cultural tensions in the scripted classroom: The value of the subjugated perspective. *Urban Education, 29*(4), 410–442.

Gutierrez, K., Rymes, B., and Larson, J. (1995). Script, counterscript, and underlife in the classroom: James Brown versus *Brown v. Board of Education. Harvard Educational Review, 65*(3), 445–471.

Harrington, S. (1987). How educators can help children of the road. *Instructor, 97,* 36–39.

Hess, R. D., & Holloway, S. D. (1984). Family and school as educational institutions. In R. Parke (Ed.), *Review of child development research.* Vol. 7. (pp. 179–222). Chicago: Univ. of Chicago Press.

Hirano-Nakanishi, M. (1986). The extent and relevance of pre-high school attrition and delayed education for Hispanics. *Hispanic Journal of Behavioral Sciences, 8*(1), 61–76.

Hirsch, B. J. (1981). Social networks and the coping process: Creating personal communities. In B. H. Gottlieb (Ed.), *Social networks and social support* (pp. 149–170). Beverly Hills, CA: Sage.

Hondagneu-Sotelo, P. (1994). *Gendered transitions: Mexican experiences of immigration.* Berkeley: University of California Press.

Howard, J. (1990). *Getting smart: The social construction of intelligence.* Lexington, MA: The Efficacy Institute.

Huang, G. (1993, January). *Health problems among migrant farmworkers' children.* Charleston, WV: ERIC Clearinghouse on Rural Education and Small Schools. (ERIC Digest ED 357 907)

Hunter, J., & Howley, C.B. (1990). *Undocumented children in the schools: Successful strategies and policies.* Charleston, WV: ERIC Clearinghouse on Rural Education and Small Schools. (ERIC Digest ED 321 962)

Improving America's Schools Act of 1994, U.S.C.A., §1301. House Committee on Education and Labor. Available: www.ed.gov/legislation/ ESEA/toc.html

Interstate Migrant Education Council. (1987). *Migrant education: A consolidated view.* Denver, CO: Author.

Kagan, S. L. (1991). *United we stand: Collaborations for child care and early education.* New York: Teachers College Press.

Kagan, S. L., & Madsen, M. C. (1971). Cooperation and competition of Mexican-American and Anglo-American children of two ages under four instructional sets. *Developmental Psychology, 5*(32), 39.

Ladson-Billings, G., & Tate, W., IV. (1995). Toward a critical race theory of education. *Teachers College Record, 97*(1), 47–68.

Laosa, L. (1982). School, occupation, culture, and family: The impact of parental schooling on the parent-child relationship. *Journal of Educational Psychology, 74*(6), 791–827.

Leistyna, P., Woodrum, A., & Sherblom, S. A. (Eds.) (1996). *Breaking free: The*

Transformative power of critical pedagogy (Harvard Educational Review, Reprint series no. 27). City, ST: Publisher.

Levin, H. M. (1987). New schools for the disadvantaged. *Teacher Education Quarterly, 13*(4), 60–83.

Levin, H. M. (1988). Accelerated schools for disadvantaged students. *Educational Leadership, 44*(6), 19–21.

Madsen, W. (1966). *Mexican-Americans of south Texas.* New York: Holt, Rhinehart, & Winston.

Madsen, M. C. & Shapira, A. (1970). Cooperative and competitive behavior of urban Afro-American, Anglo-American, Mexican-American and Mexican village children. *Developmental Psychology, 3*(1), 16–20.

McDermott, R. P. (1989). Making dropouts. In H. T. Trueba, L. Spindler, & S. Spindler (Eds.), *What do anthropologists have to say about dropouts?* (pp. 16–26). New York: Falmer Press.

McLaren, P. (1995). *Critical pedagogy and predatory culture.* New York: Routledge.

McLaren, P. (1997). *Revolutionary multiculturalism: Pedagogies of dissent for the new millennium.* Boulder, CO: Westview Press.

McLaren, P., & da Silva, T. (1993). Decentering pedagogy: Critical literacy, resistance and the politics of memory. In P. McLaren & P. Leonard (Eds.), *Paulo Freire: A critical encounter* (pp. 47–89). New York: Routledge.

Meisels, S., Dorfman, J. A., & Steele, D. (1992). *Contrasting approaches to assessing young children's school readiness and achievement.* Washington, DC: National Center for Educational Statistics, U.S. Department of Education.

Middleton, C. R. (1987). Teaching the thundering herd: Surviving in a large classroom. In M. A. Shea (Ed.), *On teaching, Vol. I* (p. 13–24). Boulder: Faculty Teaching Excellence Program, University of Colorado.

Migrant Student Record Transfer System. (1992). *FTE and student distribution summary, January 1–December 31, 1992.* Little Rock, AR: Author.

Migrant Student Record Transfer System. (1994). *FTE and student distribution summary, January 1–December 31, 1994.* Little Rock, AR: Author.

Moll, L. (1990). Introduction. In L. Moll (Ed.), *Vygotsky and education: Instructional implications and applications of sociohistorical psychology* (pp. 1–27). Cambridge, MA: Cambridge University Press.

National Center for Education Statistics (1989). *Dropout rates in the United States: 1988.* Washington, DC: U.S. Government Printing Office.

National Commission on Migrant Education (1992). *Invisible children: A portrait of migrant education in the United States: Final report.* Washington, DC: U.S. Government Printing Office.

National Commission on Secondary Education for Hispanics (1984). *Making something happen.* Washington, DC: Hispanic Policy Development Project.

National Council of La Raza (1992). *State of Hispanic American 1991: An overview.* Washington, DC: National Council of La Raza.

Noddings, N. (1988, December). Schools face crisis in caring. *Education Week, 8*(14), 32.

Noddings, N. (1992). *The challenge to care in schools: An alternative approach to education.* New York: Teachers College Press.

Oakes, J. (1985). *Keeping track: How schools structure inequality.* New Haven, CT: Yale University Press.

Orfield, G., Bachmeier, M. James, D., & Eitle, T. (1997, September). Deepening segregation in American public schools. *Equity and Excellence in Education, 30*(2).

Orfield, G., & Eaton, S. E. (Eds.). (1996). *Dismantling desegregation: The quiet reversal of* Brown v. Board of Education. New York: New Press.

Padilla, A. M. (Ed.). (1980). *Acculturation: Theory, models, and some new findings.* Boulder, CO: Westview.

Padilla, A. M. (1986). Acculturation and stress among immigrants and later generation individuals. In D. Frick & H. Hoefert (Eds.), *The quality of urban life: Social, psychological, and physical conditions.* Berlin, Germany: Walter de Gruyter.

Parra, P. A., & Guarnaccia, P. (1995). Ethnicity, culture, and resiliency in caregivers of a seriously mentally ill family member. In H. I. McCubbin, E. A. Thompson, A.I. Thompson, and J. E. Fromer (Eds.), Resiliency in ethnic minority families. Vol. 1: Native and immigrant American Families (pp. 431–450). Madison, WI: University of Wisconsin.

Patthey-Chavez, G. (1993). High school as an arena for cultural conflict and acculturation for Latino angelinos. *Anthropology and Education Quarterly, 24*(1), 33–60.

Patton, M. Q. (1990). *Qualitative evaluation and research methods* (2nd ed.). Newbury Park, CA: Sage.

Portes, A. (1996). Introduction: Immigration and its aftermath. In A. Portes (Ed.), *The new second generation* (pp. 1–7). New York: Russell Sage Foundation.

Prewitt-Díaz, J. O., Trotter, R., & Rivera, V. (1989). *The effects of migration on children: An ethnographic study.* Harrisburg: Pennsylvania Department of Education, Division of Migrant Education.

Rosenthal, A. S., Milne, A. M., Ellman, F. M., Ginsburg, A. L., & Baker, K. A. (1983). A comparison of the effects of language background and socioeconomic status on achievement among elementary school children. In K. Baker & A. de Kanter (Eds.), *Bilingual education: A reappraisal of federal policy* (pp. 87–111). Lexington, MA: Lexington Books.

Rumberger, R. W. (1983). Dropping out of high school: The influence of race, sex, and family background. *American Educational Research Journal, 20*(2), 199–220.

Rumberger, R. W. (1987). High school dropouts: A review of issues and evidence. *Review of Educational Research, 57*(2), 101–121.

Rutter, M. (1979). Protective factors in children's responses to stress and disadvantage. In M. W. Kent & J. E. Rolf (Eds.), *Primary prevention of psychopathology: Social competence in children* (vol. 3, pp. 49–74). Hanover, NH: University Press of New England.

Rutter, M. (1984, March). Resilient children. *Psychology Today,* 57–65.

Rutter, M. (1987). Psychosocial resilience and protective mechanisms. *American Journal of Orthopsychiatry, 57*(3).

Salerno, A. (1991). *Migrant students who leave school early: Strategies for retrieval.* Charleston, WV: ERIC Clearinghouse on Rural Education and Small Schools. (ERIC Digest No. ED 335 179)

Saville-Troike, M. (1978). *A guide to culture in the classroom*. Rosslyn, VA: National Clearinghouse for Bilingual Education.

Shotland, J. (1989). *Full fields, empty cupboards: The nutritional status of migrant farmworkers in America*. Washington, DC: Public Voice for Food and Health Policy.

Shweder, R. A. (1996). True ethnography: The lore, the law, and the lure. In R. Jessor, A. Colby, & R. A. Shweder. (Eds.), *Ethnography and human development: Context and meaning in social inquiry* (pp. 15–52). Chicago: University of Chicago Press.

Smolowe, J. (1997). *An empty lap: One couple's journey to parenthood*. New York: Pocket Books.

Spindler, G. D. (Ed.). (1955). *Anthropology and education*. Stanford, CA: Stanford University Press.

Stack, C. (1974). *All our kin: Strategies for survival in a Black community*. New York: Harper & Row.

Steinberg, L., Blinde, S. L., & Chan, K. S. (1984). Dropping out among language minority youth. *Review of Educational Research, 54*(1), 113–132.

Straits, B. C. (1987, January). Residence migration and school progress. *Sociology of Education, 60*(1), 34–43.

Strang, E. W., et al. (1993). *Services to migrant children: Synthesis and program options for the Chapter 1 Migrant Education Program*. Prepared under contract for the U. S. Department of Education by Westat, Inc., Rockville, MD.

Suárez-Orozco, C., & Suárez-Orozco, M. (1995a). *Transformations: Immigration, family life and achievement motivation among Latino adolescents*. Stanford, CA: Stanford University Press.

Suárez-Orozco, C., & Suárez-Orozco, M. (1995b). Migration: Generational discontinuities and the making of Latino identities. In L. Romanucci-Ross & G. DeVos (Eds.), *Ethnic identity: Creation, conflict, and accommodation* (3rd ed., pp. 321–347). Walnut Creek, CA: AltaMira Press.

Suárez-Orozco, M. (Ed.) (1998a). *Crossings: Mexican immigration in interdisciplinary perspectives*. Cambridge, MA: Harvard University Press and D. Rockefeller Center for Latin American Studies.

Suárez-Orozco, M. M. (1998b). State terrors: Immigrants and refugees in the post-national space. In Y. Zou & H. T. Trueba (Eds.), *Ethnic identity and power: Cultural contexts of political action in school and society* (pp. 283–319). New York: State University of New York Press.

Szapocznik, J., Kurtines, W. M., & Hanna, N. (1979). Comparison of Cuban and Anglo-American values in a clinical population. *Journal of Consulting and Clinical Psychology, 47*(3), 623–624.

Taylor, P. (1934). *An American-Mexican frontier: Nueces County, Texas*. New York: Russell and Russell.

Texas Education Agency. (1997). Academic Excellence Indicator System. Available at the TEA Web site, www.tea.state.tx.us

Texas Education Agency. (1995). *Texas consolidated state plan: 1995–2000*. Austin, TX: Author.

Tharp, R. G., & Gallimore, R. (1988). *Rousing minds to life: Teaching, learning, and schooling in social context*. Cambridge, MA: Cambridge University Press.

Trueba, H. T. (1987). The ethnography of schooling. In H. T. Trueba (Ed.),

Success or failure: Linguistic minority children at home and in school (pp. 1–13). New York: Harper and Row.

Trueba, H. T. (1991). Linkages of macro-micro analytical levels. *Journal of Psychohistory, 18*(4), 457–468.

Trueba, H. T. (1997). *A Mexican immigrant community in Central California.* Unpublished manuscript, Harvard University.

Trueba, H. T. (1999). *Latinos unidos: From cultural diversity to the politics of solidarity.* Lanham, Boulder, New York, Oxford: Rowman & Littlefield.

Trueba, H. T. (2000). Interpreting Menchu's account: Sociocultural and linguistic contexts. *International Journal for Qualitative Studies in Education.*

Trueba, H. T., Cheng, L., & Ima, K. (1993). *Myth or reality: Adaptative strategies of Asian Americans in California.* London, England: Falmer Press.

Trueba, H. T., Jacobs, L., & Kirton, E. (1990). *Cultural conflict and adaptation: The case of the Hmong children in American society.* London, England: Falmer Press.

Trueba, H. T., Rodríguez, C., Zou, Y., & Cintrón, J. (1993). *Healing multicultural America: Mexican immigrants rise to power in rural California.* London, England: Falmer Press.

Trueba, H. T., & Zou, Y. (1994). *Power in education: The case of Miao university students and its significance for American culture.* London, England: Falmer Press.

Trueba, H. T., & Zou, Y. (1998). Introduction. In Y. Zou & H. T. Trueba (Eds.), *Ethnic identity and power: Cultural contexts of political action in school and society* (pp. 43–66). New York: State University of New York Press.

U.S. Bureau of the Census. (1990). www.census.us.gov.

U.S. Bureau of the Census. (1996, June). *Current population reports.* Washington, DC: U.S. Department of Commerce, Economics, and Statistics Administration.

Valdez, G. (1996). *Con respeto: Bridging the distances between culturally diverse families and schools.* New York: Teachers College Press.

Valencia, R. R. (1991). The Plight of Chicano students: An overview of schooling conditions and outcomes. In R. R. Valencia (Ed.), *Chicano school failure: An analysis through many windows* (pp. 3–26). London, England: Falmer Press.

Valverde, S. A. (1987). A comparative study of Hispanic high school dropouts and graduates: Why some leave school early and some finish? *Education and Urban Society, 19*(3), 320–329.

Vigil, D. (1989). *Barrio gangs.* Austin: University of Texas Press.

Vigil, D. (1997). *Personas Mexicanas: Chicano high schooolers in a changing Los Angeles.* In G. Spindler & L. Sprindler (Series Eds.), *Case studies in cultural anthropology.* Fort Worth, TX: Harcourt Brace College Publishers.

Villenas, S. (1996). The colonizer/colonized Chicana ethnographer: Identity, marginalization, and co-optation in the field. *Harvard Educational Review 66*(4), 711–731).

Vygotsky, L. S. (1962). *Thought and language.* Cambridge: Massachusetts Institute of Technology Press.

Vygotsky, L. S. (1978). Interaction between learning and development. In M. Cole, V. John-Teiner, S. Scribner, & E. Souberman (Eds.), *Mind in society:*

The development of higher psychological processes (pp. 79–91). Cambridge, MA: Harvard University Press.

Wallace, S. P. (1986). Central American and Mexican characteristics and economic incorporation in California. *International Migration Review, 20,* 664–668.

Werner, E., & Smith, R. (1989). *Vulnerable but invincible: A longitudinal study of resilient children and youth.* New York: Adams, Bannister, and Cox.

Werner, E., & Smith, R. (1992). *Overcoming the odds: High-risk children from birth to adulthood.* New York: Cornell University Press.

Wertsch, J. (1981). *The concept of activity in Soviet psychology.* New York: M. E. Sharpe.

Wertsch, J. (Ed.). (1985). *Culture, communication, and cognition: Vygotskian perspectives.* Cambridge, MA: Cambridge University Press.

Wertsch, J. (1991). Beyond Vygotsky: Bakhtin's contribution. In J. Wertsch (Ed.), *Voices of the mind: A sociocultural approach to mediated action* (pp. 46–66). Cambridge, MA: Harvard University Press.

Whitener, L. A. (1985). *Migrant farmworkers: Characteristics and trends.* Paper presented at the Conference on Migrant Farmworkers: Problems and Solutions, Seattle, WA.

Wilson, P. (1991). Trauma of Sioux Indian high school students. *Anthropology and Education Quarterly, 22*(4), 367–383.

INDEX

❦

ABOUT THE AUTHORS

✦

ENCARNACIÓN GARZA teaches at the University of Texas at San Antonio.

PEDRO REYES, Associate Vice Chancellor, University of Texas at Austin, is the editor of the book *Lessons from High-Performing Hispanic Schools: Creating Learning Communities* (Teachers College Press, 1999).

ENRIQUE T. TRUEBA, University of Texas at Austin, is the coauthor of *Ethnography and Schools: Qualitative Approaches to the Study of Education* (Rowman and Littlefield, 2002).